Magic of Trees & Stones

Magic of

Trees and Stones

Secrets of Japanese Gardening

by
KATSUO SAITO
and
SADAJI WADA

JAPAN PUBLICATIONS TRADING COMPANY

NEW YORK · RUTLAND · TOKYO

First Edition, 1964

Second Printing, October, 1965

Third Printing, January, 1970

Library of Congress Catalog Card No. 64–7610

Published by

Japan Publications Trading Company

175 Fifth Ave., New York, N. Y. 10010   1255 Howard Street, San Francisco, Calif. 94103

C. P. O. Box 722, Tokyo, Japan

PRINTED IN JAPAN BY DAI NIPPON PRINTING COMPANY

CONTENTS

LIST OF ILLUSTRATIONS

PREFACE

THE AUTHOR, KATSUO SAITO, IS ONE of the few Japanese garden technicians who, throughout his entire lifetime, has devoted himself to garden planning. The designing of a Japanese garden is not something that can be done from a plan alone; the designer must participate in the construction on the actual site while he creates his design. The designer must, at the same time, be a garden constructor as well. In this sense, Mr. Saito is a true garden technician. He has mastered the theories of garden design, and he is still persisting in his pursuit of good taste.

This book begins with an explanation of the characteristic shibusa of Japanese gardens, which is usually difficult for people who are not Japanese to comprehend, and goes on to treat plans for gardens as actual places to live in from an over-all housing viewpoint.

Lately, Japanese gardens have gained a good bit of respect abroad and have become a sort of fashion there. There are, however, very few garden designers who can really explain the essence of Japanese gardens. I hope that this book will be an introductory guide in the wide dissemination of the characteristic garden techniques that I earnestly desire among both garden specialists, who are delving into correct Japanese garden techniques and among general garden lovers.

TSUYOSHI TAMURA

Doctor of Forestry, Former chairman of the Japanese Institute of Landscape Architects

October, 1964

AUTHOR'S PREFACE

THOUGH THE JAPANESE GARDEN IS the child of Nature, under whose care it grows, from the very beginning it should be made clear that these gardens are not to be compared with the magnificence and mystery of all Nature. To do so would be to negate the reason for continuing on with Japanese gardens. Were our gardens merely an attempt to recreate the beauty of Nature as it is, some of the highly developed Western gardens would seem more successful to me.

What, then, is the value of the Japanese garden? If we compare Nature itself to an Adam and Eve who did not eat of the forbidden fruit, the Japanese garden can be thought of as Adam and Eve after they had eaten it and had learned to be ashamed. In other words, the Japanese garden, unlike a completely nude beauty, is a beauty who has suitably clothed her body to veil her shame. A special type of beauty, called shibusa, *or refined, quiet, tasteful beauty, has developed in Japan as that veil of modesty with which we cover the beauty of Nature. This is not the beauty of the open fields and of Nature as she is, but it is the real merit and value of the Japanese garden.*

The growing number of people in other countries who have an interest in Japanese gardens is a source of happiness to us, the garden designers. We hope that you will view our gardens as a very natural arrangement, without concentrating your attention on mere curiosity and without forming distorted interpretations, so that you will understand the meaning of the feeling of shibusa. *The photographs in this book are largely of famous gardens both old and new and were taken largely by Akira Ohira. The new works presented here were designed and executed by the Hakone Nursery Co., Ltd.*

Both Mr. Sadaji Wada, who was in charge of the photography and the plans, and I should like to express our deep appreciation to Richard L. Gage, who translated this book into English, and to the entire editorial staff of the Japan Publications Trading Company for all of their enthusiastic cooperation.

KATSUO SAITO

October, 1964

TRANSLATOR'S NOTE

As THE MAJOR CITIES OF THE WORLD grow larger, more crowded, and less pleasant to live in, people everywhere are searching for some place that is green and peaceful, for some place that brings them back into contact with Nature's healing powers, which we are in danger of losing. Cities that are better models of the dreariness of urban living than Tokyo and Osaka are, and that even Kyoto is becoming, would be difficult to find, but from ancient times, the Japanese people have been blessed with a magical ability to create, in the most cramped and unlikely urban environment, a bit of a garden that brings them back into line with values more spiritually satisfying than concrete and glass buildings and endless streams of squeeling, honking automobiles.

Though the Japanese people do bring Nature into their cities through their gardening, they do not do so in the obvious way of merely imitating a natural scene in miniature. Japanese gardening is more subtle than that. What it really does is to suggest Nature, to symbolize Nature in all her vastness, by means of a rigorously selected, meticulously placed small number of garden plants and stones that are pregnant with spiritual associations.

This sounds very high-flown and might be enough to put off an ordinary gardener who would like to emulate the miracles of Japanese gardening on his own scale, but do not be misled. The creation of these serene and elegant gardens is not accomplished by waving a magic wand over some rocks and plants and mumbling some mysterious Oriental abracadabra. It is a type of magic, but it is the magic of many years experience, careful planning, and diligent work.

There are many books on Japanese gardening that show scenes from the famous historical gardens and tell one how beautiful it all is. Mr. Saito's book, on the other hand, is not only alive to the beauty of the past, but is a rich source of taste and technical information to gardeners, Japanese and otherwise, who long to know what the magic is that will enable them to continue the great Japanese gardening traditions and to create works that will be a source of happiness and reassurance both to this spiritually battered generation and to generations to come.

RICHARD L. GAGE

October, 1964

Introduction

Shibusa, the Quiet Taste in Japanese Gardens

Shibusa, the Japanese word that means quiet and refined taste, sums up the characteristics of Japanese gardening. There are, however, shadings of meaning within the word *shibusa* itself. The *shibusa* of about A.D. 700 was light in character and might have been called elegance. Later, in about 1200, a medium grade of *shibusa* appeared that might be called mysterious or occult. Still later, in approximately 1500, we find a more intense version of *shibusa*, one that was characterized by a very quiet, subtle taste. The chart on the following page shows these three main divisions of *shibusa*.

The gardens of the light phase of *shibusa* were sunny and elegant and fell into three general categories: gardens featuring flowers and trees, those that centered around a stream, and those simple ones that featured an open lawn. The occult middle phase tended to veil splendidly beautiful natural objects with a veil of mystery in two main garden types: the grove and spring garden and the garden that used a symbolic expression of a stream or body of water where there was actually no water at all. *Shibusa* in its most intense phase, in which great stress is on the subtle and highly refined, appears in the tea gardens and in the gardens of the *sukiya-zukuri* style. Generally speaking, all of these gardens were symbolic and conventionalized.

Ancient Japanese gardens used small trees and grasses of the mountains and fields because these plants showed a great respect for sunlight. An important point in these gardens was the beauty and the profit that sunlight could bring into human life, and designers let the light into the gardens in abundance.

This was not only pleasurable and healthful, but was also socially candid and demonstrated the magnanimity of the personalities of the people who owned the garden. In the poem anthology *Manyoshu*, from A.D. 800, we find this poem:

The diagram structure:

Shibusa in the Japanese Garden branches into three categories, which all connect to **Symbolic expression**:

Elegance (light-phase *shibusa*, brightness with a touch of the quiet taste)
- Flower and tree garden (lightness of feeling, featuring flowers and grasses of mountains and fields, with trees and stones). Example: The flower and tree garden in the picture scroll of the *Tale of Genji*.
- Garden with a stream (featuring a refreshing stream of water). Example: Murin-an Garden, Kusakawa-machi, Nanzen-ji, Sakyo-ku, Kyoto.
- Open-lawn garden (featuring the simple feeling of the edges and paths of the open fields). Example: Nishi Sanso Garden, Nijuku, Yoda-mura, Kuji-gun, Ibaragi Prefecture.

The mysterious (middle-phase *shibusa*, beauty veiled in quiet taste)
- Grove and spring garden (symbolic landscape with all its brilliance muted). Example: Katsura Detached Palace Garden, Katsura, Ukyo-ku, Kyoto.
- Mountain and waterless-stream garden (stones and sand symbolizing mountains or a garden that symbolizes water where there is none). Examples: Daitoku-ji garden and Daisen-in Garden, Daitoku-ji-machi, Murasakino, Kamikyo-ku, Kyoto.

Refined simplicity (dark-phase *shibusa* perfected)
- Tea Garden (a garden for the tea ceremony with all its colors and materials dictated by the needs of the ceremony). Example: Omote Senke Roji, Tera-no-uchi-agaru, Ogawa-dori, Kamikyo-ku, Kyoto.
- *Sukiya-zukuri* garden (a garden that features the tastes for elegant simplicity, though made to suit other ideals). Example: Shisendo Garden, Ichijo-ji-machi, Sakyo-ku, Kyoto.

Symbolic expression

I have substituted modern examples of these garden types where there are no suitable ones that have come down from antiquity. The table has no connection with the periods of construction.

Villagers of Nara, hasten to see our garden,
While the clover is still in bloom.

Since in the gardens of that time a plant such as the bush clover, or even the pine which also lets in a good deal of sunlight, would be selected over luxuriant trees that block the sun, we can imagine that these gardens were very bright and sunny. The owner of

Flower and tree garden.

the garden in the poem, by sending out a call to all of the townspeople of Nara indiscriminately to come to see the clover blooming in his garden, demonstrates his democratic personality.

Though the ancient gardens of Japan showed a predilection for brightness and sunshine, they also featured light flowers like the clover and *unohana* brought from the mountains and fields, rather than richly beautiful peonies and dahlias, because the simpler flowers were admired for their feeling of light *shibusa*, or in other words, for the elegance that was typical of the gardens of those days.

The freshness of flowing water in the gardens that centered on a stream also contributed to this sense of elegance, as did the selection of such simple things as corners of fields, and field paths in the open-lawn gardens. Even if there was a sense of sorrow in these gardens, it was not intended to be serious sorrow, but was only there to point up the elegance of this simple refinement.

The ancient gardens began by reflecting the magnificence of Nature on a grand scale, but later when it became clear that it was too much to attempt to force this grandeur into a limited space, techniques developed to reduce the waste in the complexity of Nature and to extract the essence of its beauty. In other words, designs began to symbolize the atmosphere of natural beauty in the idealization of groves and fountains. These precepts were written down long ago in the twelfth-century classic on gardening, *Sakuteiki*, where methods are mentioned whereby one could collect together the essential points of a landscape into a small space to create a desired effect. Moreover, there is also a method for symbolizing water, through the magic of plants and stones, in places where there is actually no water at all. This is not a means of openly presenting the feeling of water through stones, or through stones, sand, plants, and trees. It is rather a profound example of refined *shibusa*. It also is not merely an instance of arranging appealing beautifully colored stones in such a way that they are half hidden, half revealed by the vegetation. It is more like covering with a film objects, perhaps crude before, so that they acquire a graceful, quiet beauty, twice as beautiful, twice as profound, and

*Garden with
a stream.*

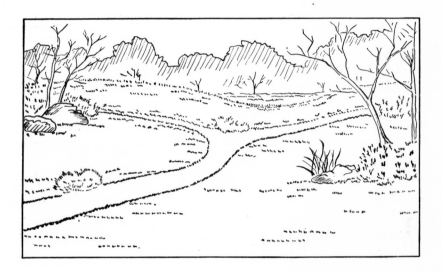

Open-lawn garden.

much more mysterious than their own frank beauty could have been. This is an example of the medium *shibusa*, or a feeling of mystery, in which there are many instances of concealing the apparent beauty of objects so that they gain a certain serenity and a sense of the occult.

Mysterious beauty has a number of expressions, and since it is mainly used in gardens and in the Noh drama in traditional Japanese arts, it is regarded as difficult to understand. At the risk of seeming excessive, I should like to interject one more example.

Though a naked woman is certainly beautiful, if she is covered in some thin veiling, her beauty is greatly enhanced. A stone, partially concealed by the foliage, presents much the same type of situation. Understanding this is the first step on the road to the mystery of refined gardening.

Although there is not much half-naked dancing in today's Kabuki, the female impersonators spare nothing to

Grove and spring garden.

Mountain and waterless-stream garden.

create the impression of charming feminity. Moreover, when they express grief, they shed copious tears and raise their voices in loud sobbing. On the other hand, in the Noh drama, not only are there no charming female creatures, but the actors rely solely on maidenly gentleness to express their beauty. When the Noh actor expresses grief, he merely raises his hand to his face and turns his face slightly downward. This symbolizing of the entire emotion of sorrow through a gesture, known as the downcast look of grief, and the symbolizing of an atmosphere, as in the waterless streams in gardening, are both outstanding examples of the mysterious in Japanese art. It is difficult to explain in concrete terms just what this occult refinement in *shibusa* is, but it alone is truly profound.

In the fifteenth century, under the influence of Buddhism, particularly Zen Buddhism and the tea ceremony, the Japanese people acquired a taste for a

Tea garden.

Sukiya-zukuri *garden.*

refined simplicity aimed at harmonious human relations and simple refinement. It was this taste that brought *shibusa* to its most intense stage and gave birth to the tea garden and the *sukiya-zukuri* garden.

The philosophic frame of mind, which after Sen-no Rikyu became the main purpose of the tea ceremony, consists of a mental attitude in which people in mutual humility, esteem each other as equals and an atmosphere in which people, using various manners and movements, embody this attitude in tastes for the tearoom, tea utensils, and the tea garden. In short this attitude is expressed in subdued tastes for quiet elegance.

Gaudy shapes and colors, specifically red or pink, pointed rocks, even high voices, and spacious areas are diametrically opposed to the feeling of refined simplicity. The garden in this style must be simple. Though a red stone partially hidden by the trees gives a sense of refinement and mystery, it is not sufficiently refined for a tea garden. It tends more to fit the style of an ordinary garden. A tea garden requires white, pale lavender or pale green small flowers, green or gray mosses, lichens, and grasses, and brown banded tree trunks that all blend into a subtle color scheme. Also necessary are low irregular prostrate stones that project only a little above the surface of the ground, the moss, or the grass, the quiet sound of a stream or of water on the boil, sunlight filtered through the trees, and a small place with a rustic air.

This feeling of quiet tastefulness calls for restraint in the company of others. Teamasters prefer a judith that only half opens and retains a sense of restraint to one that blooms full and uninhibited, because these men love the half closed, meek, and unobtrusive flowers that are in keeping with refinement. Continuing along this line of thought, we can see that a poor rustic building is more suitable to the required feeling than a building in a highly cultured and advanced city would be. Modern people, accustomed to the cultural life of a modern city, cannot live in this humble atmosphere without feeling something of tedium. Since, on the other hand, the concept of quiet refinement is difficult to abandon, these people are compromising by arranging a room in their spacious houses to harmonize with this sense. In these rooms, a little wood and stone imparts some of the magic needed to create the feeling of being away from the city.

Because this type of subtle garden is difficult to construct in a bright sunny place, a small garden where the sunlight is less than sufficient, or even perhaps an indoor garden, gives the right environment. Of course, if the place is too dark, plants will not grow, but a symbolic representation of a haunting waterless stream can be made from only sand and stones.

The roles these refined and quiet gardens play in the lives of people today will be the subject of our further attention.

CHAPTER TWO

The Basic Divisions
of the Garden

THE RESIDENTIAL GARDEN, the connection between the home and the highway, is divided into three sections: the front garden, which is the plane of contact with society, the kitchen garden, which is related to material everyday life, and the inner garden, which regulates air circulation and lighting and is the area of contact with natural beauty. Any garden must contain these three sections, insofar as the limits of the living space permit. The first question to be settled is the division of the land into these three basic sections. The division of the land to suit special conditions or, in case there is an extra margin of land, into supplementary and auxiliary sections is left to the tastes of the garden owner. However, auxiliary sections should not be permitted to flourish to the point where they interfere with the basic functions of the inner garden, that is regulation of light and air circulation and providing an area of contact with natural beauty.

Some of the types of auxiliary gardens that you could create are, for instance, the courtyard garden in a narrow space surrounded by buildings, gardens especially created and cultured for the interior of the house or for the rooftop, gardens devised to serve as alleyways in the narrow passages between buildings, enclosed tea gardens for tearooms included in a house, or a tea garden in the area of a tea house built independent of the main house. In addition, if there is enough land, if the owner wishes, he can construct a flower garden, an orchard, a vegetable garden, an archery gallery, a golf training course, tennis courts, volleyball courts, animal pens, or any variety of miscellaneous auxiliary sections to use up vacant space. Of course, these auxiliary garden sections enrich daily living, but their absence is not particular hindrance (*Figure 1*).

The following chart shows how the divisions of the garden can be made to reflect the basic sections related to

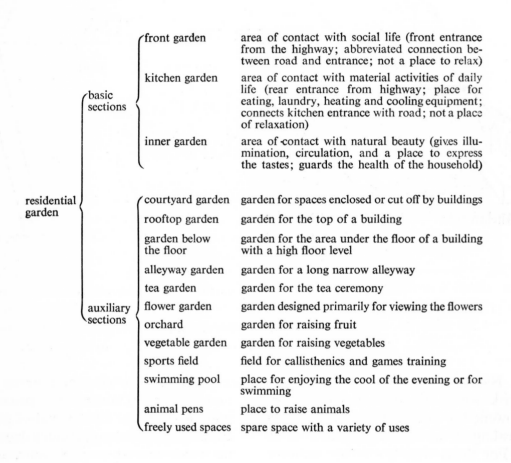

		front garden	area of contact with social life (front entrance from the highway; abbreviated connection between road and entrance; not a place to relax)
residential garden	basic sections	kitchen garden	area of contact with material activities of daily life (rear entrance from highway; place for eating, laundry, heating and cooling equipment; connects kitchen entrance with road; not a place of relaxation)
		inner garden	area of contact with natural beauty (gives illumination, circulation, and a place to express the tastes; guards the health of the household)
	auxiliary sections	courtyard garden	garden for spaces enclosed or cut off by buildings
		rooftop garden	garden for the top of a building
		garden below the floor	garden for the area under the floor of a building with a high floor level
		alleyway garden	garden for a long narrow alleyway
		tea garden	garden for the tea ceremony
		flower garden	garden designed primarily for viewing the flowers
		orchard	garden for raising fruit
		vegetable garden	garden for raising vegetables
		sports field	field for callisthenics and games training
		swimming pool	place for enjoying the cool of the evening or for swimming
		animal pens	place to raise animals
		freely used spaces	spare space with a variety of uses

the plan of the house and the auxiliary sections.

If the front garden and the kitchen garden are made to face directly onto the road they become useless, and the private areas in them will inevitably vanish.

The inner garden is indispensable as a free and unlimited source of light and pure air. It is very important to the healthfulness of the environment and to the enrichment of human life. Moreover, from the viewpoint of taste, it serves as a mirror reflecting the pleasures of the vast world of Nature. If there were only buildings and no gardens, we might never see the bright harvest moon or experience the joy, the melody, and the poetry that come from the beauty God gives to all men

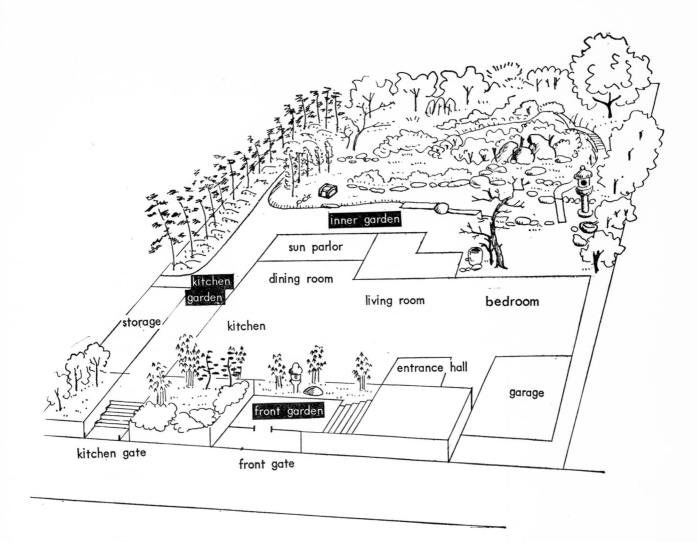

Figure I. Basic divisions of the garden.

in Nature's gentle spring breezes, the brisk winds of autumn, the colorful flowers, the falling red leaves, and the rustling of the trees above.

For those who live in the country, in the mountains, by a lake, or at the seaside, these places in themselves are natural gardens. Nevertheless, perhaps even beyond this, it is better to devise a method of merely guaranteeing the harmony that is inherent in a place for individual living. The method of guaranteeing this harmony certainly depends upon the care taken in the gardening. For instance, this aim can be achieved by careful placing of the plants and by limiting the plants so that they do not damage the natural scenery.

PART ONE:
The General Garden

The Front Garden
and
The Kitchen Garden

§1 *Function and Essentials of the Front Garden*

MORE than just an entrance and exit to the front of the house, the front garden serves to impart a feeling of initimacy and dignity to the entrance-way. The best approach to follow in the front garden is to moderate the strictness of the *shibusa* tastes rather than attempt to fruitlessly magnify the garden's importance or attempt to make it look meaner than it is. Since the front garden is the link between the road and the entrance of the house, it is a convenient location, and it is not often possible to choose where one would like to put it. Insofar as it is possible, it is most advantageous to arrange the inner garden, which requires sunlight, on the southeast and to put the front garden on the north or west. (This pertains to the northern hemisphere.)

In a case where the houses are lined up adjacent along a street, it is a good idea to make the front garden fence low, or do away with it altogether, and create the appearance of one long continuous front garden.

If the front garden is to be an entrance and exit passage for people who are getting on in years, the path from the road to the entrance should be short. If it is not short, make it look as short as possible by avoiding planting tall trees and by directing the path through lawn and flowers so as to create the appearance of intimacy and easy passage. On the other hand, if yours is a home where too much coming and going is not welcome, you could give your front garden a less inviting look to the pushy salesman by making the path from the road to the entrance longer or, even if it is short, by making it curve or incline, by elevating the base of the entrance itself, or by planting in such a way as to half conceal the entrance. In other words, give it a touch of *shibusa.*

It is permissible to add touches of interest to the front garden with such things as stone lanterns, well cribs, pots, sculpture, and water basins, but there are also certain essential things in a front garden like the name plate, the mail box, and boxes for the newspaper and other delivered items, some sort of illumination, lawn sprinklers, and in some cases a parking place for the family car.

§2 *Examples of Front Gardens*

The photograph of large and small stones was taken in the front garden of the Yanase Motors Co. Hall (*Figure 2*). Because the building faces directly on a wide road, rocks and greenery were arranged between the two entrances to create a genial feeling. Large trees were avoided, not only because they would shade the building, but also because they might spoil the beauty of the building's exterior. On the left approach there is a large stone with smaller stones arranged around its base, much like calves being watched over by the mother cow. Around this is spread Shirakawa gravel. The large stone was placed on the left because it inclines to the right and makes the spirit of the garden seem to move to the right. This placement of the stone also balances the open space on the right, which as a result of the incline on the left, seems to be larger.

The azaleas and aloes around the bases of the stones add a touch of softness to the arrangement.

The photograph of pruned flowering shrubbery and trees (*Figure 3*) was taken in the front garden of the Harumi International Fair. In a corner of a spacious lawn, pruned shrubbery such as the azalea, the daphne, and *dodan* are concentrated to create volume to balance the large building. The tone of the pruned shrubs is picked up in the gentle unobtrusive undulations of the lawn. Although there are only three trees in the lawn that backs the pruned shrubbery, they blend with the over-all scene and add just the right feeling of grandeur. The evergreen pruned shrubbery is lovely, but for the four changing seasons, planting was designed to provide the fresh new green of spring, the flowering summer plants, and the bright reds and yellows of the autumn leaves.

§3 *Function and Essentials of the Kitchen Garden*

The function of the kitchen garden is to make work connected with material life easier and more efficient. Just as the front garden is used to connect the front entrance of the house with the front road, the kitchen garden connects the rear of the house with the rear road. Although such things as taste, style, and refinement cannot be said to be useless in the kitchen garden, they are definitely second considerations. It is sufficient if the kitchen garden provides a passage to the rear road, because this is its prime purpose.

If we compare ordinary living activities with the stage, the kitchen garden might be called the dressing room, or the preparations room, where things that you could not put on the stage— that is in the front or inner gardens— can be conveniently collected and controlled. However, in recent times there has been a marked tendency to put such things as cleaning equipment, clothes lines, and storage places in a part of the inner garden, under the floor of the building, in the basement, or on the building roof because this improves the passage from the kitchen door through the kitchen garden. A second essential in planning the kitchen garden is to control it in such a way that it can be maintained easily from a viewpoint of sanitation and safety, because if it is large and a great deal of everyday items are stored in it, so that it is not something to look at and enjoy, it can become very littered and dirty. Moreover, it is good to select a place without extremely strong sunlight to keep stored foods from spoiling. In the ordinary kitchen garden there must be storage space, clothes lines, a septic tank, rubbish containers, water lines, lighting, cleaning equipment, and fuel storage all compactly arranged, in addition to various equipment connected with food, heating, and cooling, and other machinery located conveniently to the back door to make work easier. It is also desirable to leave a little space for the children to play in. Kitchen gardens will vary in scale according to the lives of the residents of the house, but if they are too spacious they can cause unnecessary work.

Since the kitchen garden is a simple arrangement we will omit an example.

Figure 2.   Stone arrangement in the front garden of the Yanase Motors Hall.

Figure 3.
Pruned flowering shrubbery and
trees in the front garden of the
Harumi International Fair.

CHAPTER TWO

The Inner Garden

§1 *Function and Essentials of the Inner Garden*

THE INNER GARDEN serves the practical function of efficiently regulating the light in the living room, reception room, and bedrooms and of letting fresh clean air into the house. It may also sometimes be a sunny auxiliary living room under the blue sky with the shade of the trees and the flowers near by. All of these features of the inner garden enhance the healthfulness of the environment. In times of disaster, such as fire, heavy winds, or earthquake, the inner garden provides a certain amount of temporary shelter. As a place to live with Nature, it provides both the family and guests, even while remaining indoors, with an opportunity to enjoy natural beauty and the changing of the seasons as if they were on a stage. For these reasons it is essential to place the inner garden on the south, east, or southeast of the house (in the northern hemisphere).

As we have mentioned, there are many types of Japanese gardens, including the tree and plant garden, the stream garden, the lawn garden, the garden featuring artificial mountains, groves, and springs, the stone and sand garden, and others, but all of them, to give a sense of spaciousness, are divided into three basic parts. These parts are the foreground, the middle ground, and the background.

The foreground, depending on the position of the trees and the shade, regulates the sunlight and, by permitting a view of the middle ground and background through the trees, makes the garden look deeper. It also adds a pleasant touch in that the odors of the flowers planted there can drift into the house.

The middle ground, the main point of artistic pleasure in the garden because it is a symbolic representation of natural scenery, is developed through the use of such garden elements as a spacious lawn or body of water, a stream, or a stone and sand garden. If the garden is too small or is insufficiently lighted for trees and lawns to grow well, the owner may, depending on his tastes, use a sand and stone arrangement, a stone and moss arrangement, or a combination of the two.

The background of the garden serves as a backdrop for the middle ground and features trees and shrubs, standing stones or a pagoda, or some other element that emphasizes its sense of distance. It is also possible to incorporate scenery from beyond the garden into the background, but this will tend to eliminate the garden background and may even dominate the scene to such an extent that the garden becomes nothing but the foreground and the outside scenery. In such cases, if the background scenery beyond the garden is the sea or a lake, the front area of the garden should be a lawn or an expanse of sand. If it is mountains or hills, leave the front garden open to create a good view. If the garden is too small, plant a few trees so that the view of the sea, mountains, lake, river, or fields can be glimpsed through them.

If there is a teahouse in the inner garden, plan a tea garden in its vicinity. Even if there is not a teahouse, if the owner wishes, a tea-style garden might be used, as might any number of the auxiliary sections we have mentioned previously.

Trees to control the lighting and shade are essential to an inner garden. If the garden is spacious, you might include a summer house and benches for relaxation, a barbecue pit and tables for outdoor meals or refreshments, and illumination for viewing the garden at night. Watering equipment is needed for a garden of 30 square yards or more. Bridges, pagodas, stone lanterns, sculpture, sundials, fountains, wall springs, waterfalls, wells, water basins, and the like provide interesting accents, depending on the size of the garden and the owner's tastes; however, they should be used in moderation.

The inner garden may be as gorgeous as the owner wishes, but *shibusa* and the hint of the mysterious that comes from veiling the obviously beautiful are very important in preserving the dignity of the garden.

§2 *Various Foreground Arrangements*

A Stone for the Shoes

Since in Japan it is the custom to remove one's shoes before entering the house, in the front of the veranda of a Japanese house there is usually a stone on which to leave the shoes. This stone is also important in making coming in and going out of the house easier because it acts as a suitable modulation among the heights of the garden base, the floor of the house, and the floor of the veranda. Moreover, because in a visual sense, it acts as a connective between the garden and the interior, it should be set with this in mind.

The shoe stone should be about four inches narrower than the depth of the eave and less than three tenths of the frontage width of the opening or of the veranda. If the stone is wider than the eave is deep, it will get wet when it rains, and if it is five to seven tenths of the width of the opening of the veranda it will be too imposing and will overwhelm the opening itself. On the other hand, if one is willing to overlook the splashing of the rain on the broader stones, they are more comfortable. Though the heights of the garden base, the veranda floor, and the house floor may vary considerably, human legs are all more or less of a sort, and if the floor of the veranda is low, one stone will suffice. If, on the other hand, the floor is higher, you should make a sort of stairstep arrangement with a second or even a third stone step. If the veranda floor height is twelve inches or so, one stone will be sufficient, if it is set so that its top surface is ten inches below the veranda level and two inches above the level of the garden. Since the shoe stone is about the same height as stepping stones, if the stepping stones begin

at the edge of the veranda, a shoe stone may be unnecessary.

It is usual to go up to the veranda of a house, just as one would mount a staircase, where the ordinary suitable rise is from six to eight inches. In a Japanese house, however, because people often sit on the veranda floor with both feet on the shoe stone and because if one's knees rise up in too sharp an angle when sitting the skirt of a Japanese *kimono* will become messy and spoil one's appearance, the shoe stone is usually set so that its top surface is ten to twelve inches below the floor level. The difference in heights between the second and third steps can be the same as the ordinary rise in a staircase, that is, six to eight inches. The usual shoe stone, other than in a teahouse, extends directly up to the groundwork and enters under the veranda floor to penetrate the small supporting pillar which does not extend above the veranda floor. The photograph illustrating the stone for the shoes (*Figure 4*) is an example of this type setting. Because the floor level is low, one stone is plenty. The photograph illustrating shoe stones set in a zigzag pattern (*Figure 5*) shows rectangular *Katsura* stones joined and set. In this case, also, because the veranda is low, one step is enough. The stone in front of the stone for the shoes is a stepping stone. Because this open veranda, which is exposed to the rain, is

Figure 4. Stone for the shoes.

Figure 5. Shoe stones set in a zigzag pattern.

lower than the ordinary veranda, again, only one shoe stone is needed.

B   Under the Eaves

The area under the eaves may be lined off with a straight line of small stones and then filled in with uniform gravel as in Figure 4, or it may be spread with a compound mortar made of weathered granite sand in three parts to one part cement and given slightly rounded borders. Use of gravel set in cement often results in an uninteresting rigid feeling. It is also possible to pave this area with concrete finished with motar so that it resembles flag stones with a border of rectangular stones as in Figure 6, but this is a method suitable to shrine and temple architecture and is too stiff and uninteresting for the ordinary garden.

As in Figure 7, illustrating the rain gutter, the outer edge of the eaves area could be bordered with edging stones to form a sort of gutter, and then the area could be filled in with gravel or bits of tile in a uniform size of about one inch. This arrangement prevents the falling rain from making holes in the earth.

Figure 8 shows another rain gutter with small stones arranged neatly together to form a straight line. This also is a formal and elegant eaves arrangement.

Figure 6 (above).
Eaves area paved with square stones.

Figure 7 (left).
Rain gutter with gravel.

Figure 8 (right).
Rain gutter with small flat stomes.

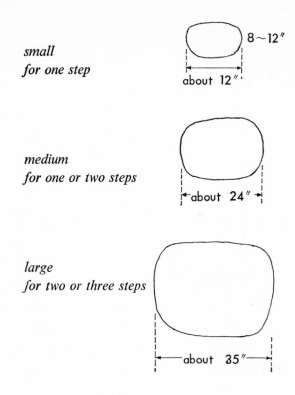

small
for one step

8~12″

about 12″

medium
for one or two steps

about 24″

large
for two or three steps

about 35″

Stepping Stone Sizes

C Stepping Stones

Because the marks left by shoes and other footwear on the surface of the garden would be unsightly, flat stepping stones, like those in Figure 9, provide adequate passage but are arranged at fairly wide but easy to cross intervals to give a feeling of light grace. Stones in this sort of arrangement are called *tobi-ishi* or "skipping stones" in Japanese. Usually the interval between such stones is about four inches. The gardener will choose as a standard width a stone on which he can put his foot in a sideways position. Although, from the viewpoint of easy walking, the ideal would be to take as a basic distance the interval between the footprints left by the natural walking of someone in the garden, since there will be scenery to stop and look at, four inches seems a good norm.

Although, depending on the gardener, stepping stones may be set at as narrow an interval as two inches, because an essential sense of nimbleness and simplicity is the aesthetic life of stepping stones, too close a setting is not admirable. There is a school of gardening in the northeast of Japan in which the stepping stones are set at from 16 to 20 inches apart, but when the stones are wet or covered with ice the long strides required to walk on such stones make slipping and falling dangerously possible. Such individual tastes as this, however, do not constitute a gardening norm.

Since, generally speaking, stepping stones are to walk on, they begin in such places as the stone for shoes in the front of the veranda or at a dividing path and end at, say, a gate or a bridge. In instances where you must decide to use one stone too few, which would make the arrangement too open, or one stone too many, which would tend to crowd the arrangement, use one stone too many. Even though overcrowding the arrangement means some of the light grace of the stones will be lost, if the stones are too widely separated, walking

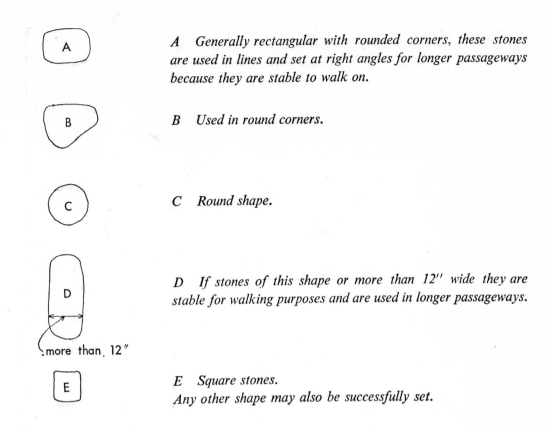

A   Generally rectangular with rounded corners, these stones are used in lines and set at right angles for longer passageways because they are stable to walk on.

B   Used in round corners.

C   Round shape.

D   If stones of this shape or more than 12″ wide they are stable for walking purposes and are used in longer passageways.

E   Square stones.
Any other shape may also be successfully set.

Stepping Stone Shapes

on them may be dangerous.

Stones of a diameter of approximately twelve inches are the best to express the feeling of lightness that is essential to the stepping stone; however, aside from the large stepping stones used in spacious gardens, it is sometimes desirable to use large stones of a diameter of one or two yards near the house to add a touch of grandeur to the distant scenery. In such cases, because preserving the lightness of the arrangement is as important as adding the touch of magnificence, the interval between the stones may be widened or shortened as long as doing so does not make walking on the stones difficult.

The height of the stone from the surface of the ground to the top of the stone is usually about two inches, but since a lower setting is less dangerous and a higher setting might be more attractive, the stones should be set at the discretion of the owner of the garden.

There are various ways of arranging the stones in patterns so that they are easy to walk on. For large- and medium-size stones you might choose a straight line plan in keeping with the scenery system of the garden, or a bent "V" pattern or an "S" curve. Stones can also be placed in a staggered arrangement with a series of four stones in a straight line alternating with a series of either three or two stones in a straight line

Height of stones from
surface of ground

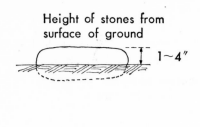

1~4"

*If the appearance of
the stone is primary a
high setting is better;
if safety is the main
aim a low setting is
preferable.*

Distance between Stepping Stones

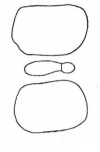

*Large and medium
stepping stones should
be set far enough
apart to put your foot
sideways between
them and have a little
room left over.*

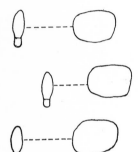

*Small stones should
be positioned at the
distance there is be-
tween normal foot-
prints.*

Stepping stones

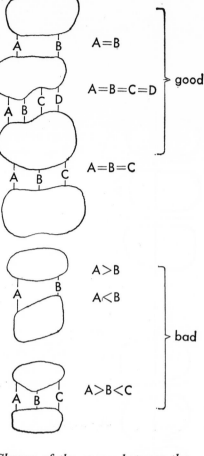

A=B

A=B=C=D

} good

A=B=C

A>B

A<B

} bad

A>B<C

*Shapes of the spaces between the
stones.
It is not necessary to set round
stones as we have shown above.*

slightly to the side of the four-stone series, so that in walking along one must take a step to the side. Because stones of a diameter of under twelve inches arranged in a straight line give the uncomfortable walking sensation of walking over logs, they should be arranged in a pattern staggered to suit the ordinary right-left of the normal walking gait. The four stones in the foreground of Figure 9 are arranged in this way. The normal footstep pattern is usual in the *sukiya*-style gardens which mainly employ small stepping stones. As you can see, this arrangement is most successful in expressing the light feeling of stepping stones.

Adjacent stones can be arranged with parallel facing edges in such a way that if the end of one stone juts out in one direction, the end of the neighboring stone will jut out in the opposite direction. This method is used to form a curved line. The stones in the upper section of Figure 9 and the first four stones in the lower section are arranged in this fashion. This is the normal arrangement, but as an exception, the fifth, sixth, seventh, and eighth stones from the bottom in the same figure and all of the stones in Figure 10 are completely unparallel. Bends in stepping stones, aside from the deliberately ornamental type in Figure 10, are always safe to use.

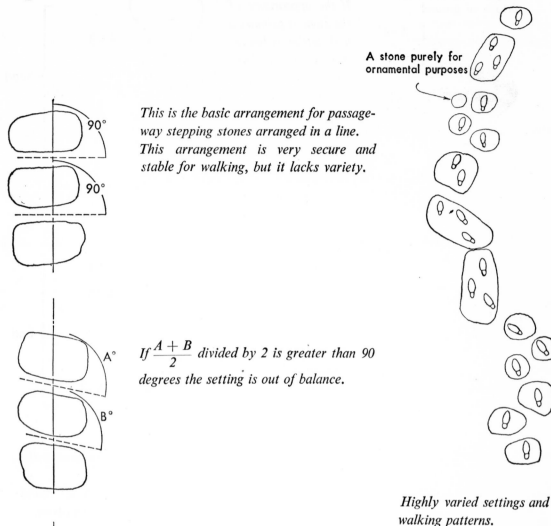

This is the basic arrangement for passageway stepping stones arranged in a line. This arrangement is very secure and stable for walking, but it lacks variety.

A stone purely for ornamental purposes

If $\dfrac{A + B}{2}$ divided by 2 is greater than 90 degrees the setting is out of balance.

If $\dfrac{A + B}{2}$ equals 90 degrees the setting is good. This type of setting has variety and the stability of the basic setting.

Highly varied settings and walking patterns.

For variation in the appearance of stepping stones, they can be mixed with rectangular stones as in Figures 11 and 12, an interesting pattern can be made with block stones arranged horizontally and vertically as in Figure 13, or long slender stepping stones treated like rec-

tangular stones can be mixed with a pavement-style arrangement as in Figure 14. The combination of rectangular stones and stepping stones in Figure 12 and the oblong stones and paving stones in Figure 14 are examples of really skilful arranging, but they are more suitable to a garden that is focused on quiet, simple tastes than to an open and imposing garden.

Suitable materials for stepping stones are such stones as granite, diorite, and other rough textured stones of a subtle coloring that will take moss well. Red stones are too gorgeous and not sufficiently relaxing to be used.

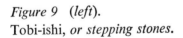
Figure 9 (left).
Tobi-ishi, or stepping stones.

Figure 10 (above).
Formal stepping-stone
arrangement.

Figure 11 (right).
Rectangular and natural
stepping stones.

Figure 12.
Stepping stones set in moss.

Figure 13.
Block stepping stones.

Figure 14.   Round stepping stones and paving stones.

D Paving Stones

Flat stones joined together to cover a given level area, or paving stones, are called *tatami* stones in Japanese after the woven straw mats which cover the floors in Japanese houses. There must naturally be a joint, or *meji*, between these stones.

Square or rectangular stones arranged as in Figure 15 are called true (*shin*) paving stones. Laying these stones in a wicker-work or herring-bone pattern with short jointing as in Figure 16 is somewhat less formal than the true paving stones, but as a variation, it is more interesting. These arrangements might be compared to very formal attire in that they are more suited to some types of homes, temples, or shrines, rather than to general garden use.

The type of paving shown in Figure 17, in which we see rectangular stones mixed with flat-topped round stones, is called abbreviated paving, or *gyo*, and if compared to clothing, might be something like a business suit or a type of formal Japanese coat called the Oshima *haori*, and is also a little smart for general gardens. The long narrow rectangular stones in these arrangements, called *tanjaku* because they are shaped like a type of vertical poetry card that was much in vogue in the Heian period, add a touch of charm whether they are used in paving or whether they are interspersed with stepping stones. In Figure 18, the informal arrangement of paving stones made up entirely of rounded stones with no rectangular stones used at all is called *so*, or grass, or sometimes, picturesquely, sprinkled hail stones. Because the paving in Figures 19 and 20 employs large flat stones but no rectangular stones, it too belongs to the *so* category and if compared to clothing might be something like the Japanese *yukata*, a light cotton lounging garment. There are various *so* pavings set staggered and without borders that suit gardens in the quiet taste. However, even if the garden is not a tea garden, stones of considerable width are exceptional. Usually the stones should be from 16 to 20 inches across. Stones of widths from one to two yards are better in restaurants or public building entrances.

When the paving is a continuation of a stepping-stone path it is most usual to set it at the same height from the ground as the stepping stones themselves, that is from 1 to $2\frac{1}{2}$ inches. When the paving is to be laid like floor tiles, the jointing should be in straight lines, but if you are going to use the wicker-work style or one of the *so* styles, avoid jointing in the shape of a cross or with two lines that intersect at right angles, and attempt to use the Y shape as a standard. Also, do not have the jointing converge in one place because this

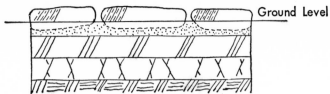

Cross Section

Ground Level

Ground Plan

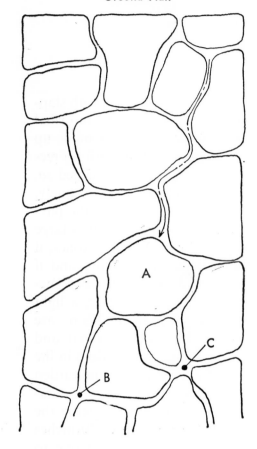

The line of crevices between the stones represented by the arrow is interrupted by stone A for a feeling of stability. The crevices should not continue in an uninterrupted line past more than three stones, or the pavement will look as if it is about to fall apart.

The intersections of the crevices at points B and C where too many crevices collect are not good.

looks overly structural and is depressing. Since jointing that passes more than three stones in a continuous line gives the impression that the pavement will break and looks weak, you should avoid it also.

In Figure 21 the paved staircase features large stones at the edges of the steps with small stones on the landings. Insofar as your garden space will permit, the step riser should be as low and the steps as wide as possible because these garden staircases are designed for comfortable strolling, not for hurried coming and going. The height of the riser should be approximately six inches, and the width of the step 12 to 20 inches if the staircase is for going up one foot at a time, and approximately 31 inches if both feet are to be placed on the same step at the same time. Too broad a step is uncomfortable to walk on one foot at a time, and too narrow a one is bad if one walks with both feet on the same step. If your garden space is limited the riser may be higher and the step narrower, but this is not recommended.

Figure 15. True (shin) paving stones.

*Figure 16.
Paving stones in wickerwork
pattern.*

Figure 17. Gyo *pavement of rectangular and round stones.*

Figure 18. So *pavement of round stones.*

Figure 19. So *pavement of large and small flat stones.*

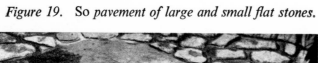

Figure 20. So-*style pavement.*

Figure 21. Paved staircase.

E The Water Basin and the Open Veranda

After sunlight, water is one of the most important things in human life. From ancient times water has been regarded as sacred in gardens in both the East and the West. It is particularly so in Japanese gardens, where pure water is brought and poured into a stone water basin to wash away the uncleanliness from the soul. This is not the type of water basin that might be found beside a lavatory for the purpose of merely washing the hands but is a part of a spiritual ritual designed to cleanse stains from the heart. In the case of the stone basin in the tea garden the conception is to purify the soul before entering the tea house, an idea born from the faith that pure undefiled water is sacred.

The *shoin*-style basin, placed beside a toilet, in Figure 22 is a slender cylindrical shape known as an *ensei-shuku*-style basin. There is another type of basin, called a bridge piling basin, which resembles this one but is somewhat different in that it has a smaller opening. The basin is usually 18 to 24 inches away from the veranda and twelve inches taller than the veranda. The slender stone standing under the veranda is called the "leaning stone," because it seems to be stooping over. It is set to lean forward towards the water

basin to serve as protection from splashing when the basin is in use. The stone near the wall on the other side of the basin is called the "cleanliness stone" and is there to spiritually conceal the ordinary unpleasantness of the toilet. That is to say, by paying attention to this stone, one can more or less forget about the toilet. The low flat stone (*mizukumi*) in front of the basin is to stand on when pouring water into the basin. The stone (*mizuage*) to the left of the partially concealed *shoin* basin in Figure 23 is to stand on when drawing the water from the basin and is set a little higher than the stone for pouring the water in. Both of these stones are called service stones. The depression in front of the basin is to prevent the water from flowing off when the basin is in use. In the center there is a drain to prevent the water's standing. I refer you to the chapter on the *tsukubai*-type water basin for the construction of drains because they are made in the same way in both cases. (*See page 192.*) You may either spread gravel in the depression in front of the basin or pave it with small round stones.

The basin in Figure 23 is a boulder shaped basin with a *kakehi* flume for conducting the water. Because the flume usually keeps pouring water into the basin without stopping, drains are absolutely essential for basins with them.

The *shoin* basin in Figure 24 is some distance away from the veranda so that

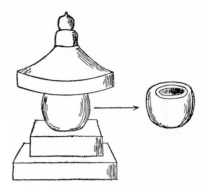

A five-storied tower and an iron-pot water basin.

one climbs onto the veranda to use it. Because the open veranda is an elegant area the center of the frame is floored with either boards, round poles, roughly adzed hexagonal poles, or sometimes with bamboo lined together as in a raft. Although this veranda is bracketed, they may also be supported on a short pillar from the ground, or they may intersect with the stone used to stand on when pouring water into the basin, or with one of the edging stones of the drainage depression. This basin, in the shape of a steel pot, was originally the middle section of a *gorin,* a stone Buddhist tower, the upper section of which fitted into the hole carved out in the basin's top. There are also copies of this type. The two long narrow bamboo poles on the top of the basin are to rest the dipper on. The so-called water catching stones in the center of the drainage pit are usually four or five stones, about four inches in diameter, arranged like floor tiles to conceal the drainage hole and to serve an ornamental purpose.

The basin in Figure 25 is partially concealed by the leaves of an orchid plant, and the service stones are not visible. The shape of the basin is the pleasant refined one of a simple bottle, but since a great deal of water will go into the basin and since such a quantity of water will sour easily, it is necessary to use the bamboo flume for a constantly fresh supply. Because the dipper on top of the basin is shallow it is turned face down; in the case of a deeper dipper, the mouth would usually face left. In this case the water overflows from the basin towards the front. There is no objection to a basin with a level edge from which the water flows more or less evenly all around the circumference of the basin; however, if there is a distortion in the rim so that you cannot control the flow of the water, place the basin so that the overflow will be in front.

Stone basins that might be used in a *shoin*-type situation or in front of an ordinary veranda include the natural stone with a water-eroded hole to contain the water or the natural boulder with only a simple hole cut for the water. This type is usually fairly high ranging from 30 to 40 inches. You might also choose any of a variety of other types such as the *kesa* type, the Ginkaku type, which is marked with geometric carvings, the jujube-shaped basin, the square basin, the slender cylindrical *enseishuku* basin, or the bridge-piling basin.

Figure 22. Shoin-*style basin.*

Figure 23. *Boulder-shaped basin.*

Figure 24.   The open veranda and a basin shaped like an iron pot.

Figure 25.   Bottle-shaped basin.

59

Ginkaku-ji basin.

Basin with four images of Buddha.

Basin with six images of Buddha.

Basin with carved moon and geese.

Saltpan basin.

Hokyointo basin.

Jujube-shaped basin.

Figure 26. *Various types of water basins.*

Enseishuku *basin.*

Iron-pot-shaped basin.

Basin in shape of sake *cup.*

Boulder-shaped basin.

Boulder-shaped basin.

Fusen *basin.*

Boulder-shaped basin.

F Other Areas around the House

Plan the trees and shrubs in your garden to act as a background for the architecture, with which it should blend to create a fresh beauty. Blending your house with your garden is very much like a conductor's blending the sounds of a variety of musical instruments into a unified and beautiful performance through the rhythm of his baton. From the beginning, an important function of the trees around the house is to control natural lighting. This will naturally depend to some extent on the equipment of the house itself, but it is better to choose deciduous trees for the areas where sunlight is needed all year round. For places near windows or at the edges of porches and verandas, it is better to plant trees with sparse branches or trees through whose branches and trunks the distant scenery provides a pleasant view from the inside of the house. A view that is partially obscured by branches and tree trunks is superior to a straight-line unobstructed view. Trees near the house look better and seem to hug the house if they incline outward into the garden. The evergreens with sparse leaves are also suitable even if they stand up straight, but if they are straight, remember it is never possible to make a properly erect tree incline.

Although it is also interesting to plant a large number of trees to give the impression that the house is standing in a forest, in Japanese gardens we usually limit ourselves to one or two trees which symbolize a forest. In addition, we usually attempt to take the plants' natural growing habitat as the standard for our garden planting. For instance, when we plant a pine, we plant the types of things under the pine that usually live well there, such as eulalia, bush clover or torch azalea. We could also spread a continuous carpet of hairmoss. If the branches of the pine are sparse, we might plant a lawn. In the cases of trees that develop high upwards, like *konara*, *soro*, or the *shidezakura*, the shrubs planted in their shade might include *gamazumi*, or the Japanese beauty berry, in addition to which we might plant mountain grasses and a lawn. If the tall trees in the arrangement are a tall bamboo like the *moso* bamboo, the plants beneath them might be something like *kakuremino* or the spear flower.

Setting too tall standing stones close to the house results in an uncomfortable arrangement which tends to upset the viewer. It is much safer to choose stones that are as low and as calm in appearance as possible.

You might also bring a pond or direct a stream near the house, but if the floors of the house are not concrete, or at least 40 inches high, do not run the stream under the house, because if you do the floor boards and, in a Japanese house, the *tatami* mats, will rot from the moisture. There is no reason why you could not leave openings between the floor boards, as you would in constructing an open veranda, to create little views downward through them.

As you can see in Figure 27 where there are too many stones near the house, although it is good that tall stones are not used, somehow or other the stones themselves are overly conspicuous. This may depend on the focal point of the photograph, but I think the garden would have been better if the stones on the bank of the dry stream arrangement in the foreground had been one quarter the size that they are and if the gravel stream bed had been narrower and the lawn more spacious.

In Figure 28 there are some Nebukawa stepping stones set near the house. These stones are well set low to the ground, and although their numerous curved lines are somewhat eye catching,

the arrangement is saved by the skill with which the stones are combined.

Figure 29 shows a fresh and harmonious arrangement in a difficult combination of a small-mouth well crib with a pond with a paving stone rim, a staircase, a lawn, and a well set scenic stone. Though in this case the horizontal planes of the lawn and the pond surface are at odds, the feeling that the expanse of water is about to overflow is successfully conveyed. This type of design was chosen, because this is a garden foreground.

The pond in Figure 30 comes in contact with the house and has stepping stones across it. I refer to this because examples of this sort occur. It is perhaps the fault of the photograph, but the stones seem small and with their rounded upper surfaces give an unstable feeling. It is better to choose stones with a perfectly flat upper surface.

Figure 27. An instance of too many stones near the house.

Figure 28. Stepping stones near the house.

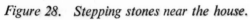

Figure 29.   Pond, well crib, and lawn.

Figure 30.
Pond with stepping stones.

§3 *Stone Arrangements*

A *Shibusa* in Stone Arrangements

In the Japanese national anthem, the first line, in expressing the wish that His Majesty the Emperor's days may continue till the gravel has grown into boulders and is covered with moss, points up an ancient Japanese feeling that moss-covered stones are the ultimate in beauty. Although an opposite opinion, to the effect that moss is a sickness in stones, also existed among the people of the past, in the final analysis, the subtle refinement, or the *shibusa*, with which moss veils the beauty of stones has found favor with the majority, and moss-covered stones are generally recognized as a very important element in the Japanese garden. This is true not only of natural stones, but also of such stone art objects as garden basins and stone lanterns, in which the texture of the stone is highly valued, and the objects themselves are much praised for a refined and subtle covering of moss.

Of course, speaking from the viewpoint of subtlety in the garden, black stones are preferable to brilliant red or blue ones; nevertheless, brightly colored stones can be used in a refined way. Avoid color contrasts between red and blue, and combine pink or lavender stones with blue stones in such a way that the arrangement seems to become blue, and place it where it can be seen through the branches of a tree. The subtle use of bright colored stones depends on the skill of the person who uses them. Stones may be gorgeous like new gold brocades, but it is when they become old that they display the composed and refined beauty of *shibusa*.

From the viewpoint of shape, stones without jagged points and edges are more refined, in much the same way that a person of sedate demeanor is more refined than one who gives vocal vent to his anger. Stones that are too knobby and bumpy, like lava, tend to be hectic and fail to give a composed impression. One should always choose stones with just the right amount of projections and undulations. Moreover, it is more refined and tasteful to use too few stones than to use too many. What we are calling *shibusa* in these cases is not something dark. Cave-like lava arragements are melancholy because the *shibusa* is overdone to the point where it is not *shibusa* in the true sense at all.

B Symbolism

It is essential to understand the symbolism in Japanese garden stone arrangements to understand the arrangements themselves. Although there are many types of symbolism in stone arranging, in general they all can be divided into the following five major groups:

Symbolism in stone arrangements
- Natural symbolism—the natural size atmosphere or larger-than-natural-size atmosphere
- Mood symbolism—personifications or abstractions of ideals
- Idea symbolism—worldly customs, religion, or world views
- Spiritual symbolism—the spirit in calm or the symbolism of vigilance, and the dynamic spirit
- Melodic symbolism—high and low or strong and weak gradually reaching a climax

As we said in Chapter One, the ancient gardeners of Japan, realizing that it was not feasible to force the magnitude of natural scenery into limited spaces, chose rather to select a few trees and stones and through them to symbolize the essence of such natural scenes as mountains, rivers, and the sea. This is not a representation of Nature but is an example of the magic of trees and stones that symbolizes the inner secrets of natural scenery. In other words, it is an example of the so-called mystery of the Japanese garden's quiet refinement that we mentioned earlier.

Though from the outset the variety of shapes of natural stones is limitless, in about 1800, stones in Japanese gardens were divided into five major categories, called the *gogyoseki*, or five natural stones. *Gogyo*, or the division of all things into five natural elements, is derived from the ancient physical and chemical learning of the Chinese, but these five natural stones have no essential connection with that learning. It is merely that the people of old, thinking that all cosmic phenomena were caused by the combining and breaking down of the five basic elements, believed life came from their combinations and variations. With this in mind, they borrowed the five Chinese letters representing these elements and applied them to the five classes of stone shapes.

If we force the coincidence and arrange the five natural stones in the same order which the Chinese used for the five natural elements—*gogyo* or wood, fire, earth, gold, and water—the *taido* stone corresponds to wood, the *shigyo* stone to fire, the *kikyaku* stone to earth, the *reisho* stone to gold, and the *shintai* stone to water. In the stone classification chart, Figure 31, the *taido* stone ranges in shape through drawings F-J. It is a forceful stone suggesting the high-rising trees. Drawings L-P show the *shigyo* stone, which branches energetically to the sides as fire does. The *kikyaku* stone, drawings U-Z, is solid like the earth and is set to seem to be a swell in the surface of the ground. Drawings A-E represent the *reisho* stone, which has the stability of gold or steel. Finally, the *shintai* stone, drawings Q-T, has the calm horizontality of water.

I have divided stones according to their shape characteristics and, from the infinite number available, have selected only twenty-six to correspond to the letters of the alphabet. The stones are arranged in five rows according to the five categories we have mentioned. Row number one contains the *reisho* stones, which gardeners popularly call principal stones. In row two are the *taido* stones called body stones. Row three contains the *shigyo* stones, called peeping stones. In row four are the *shintai* stones, which the gardeners call level base stones, and in row five there are the *kikyaku* stones, also known as root or prostrate stones.

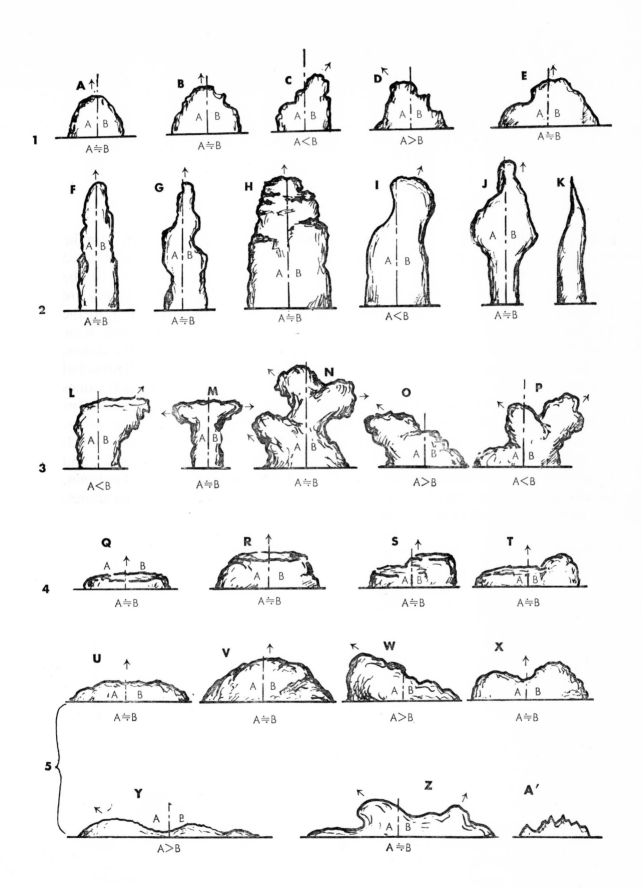

Figure 31.   Stone shape classifications.

the atmosphere of the open fields.

The atmosphere of a rough beach.

C   *Natural symbolism*

C   Natural Symbolism

The stones A-E in row one in their natural size symbolize stable standing stones, which are used in their symbolically amplified size to symbolize the atmosphere of mountains and hills. To create this atmosphere it is necessary to set these stones higher than the normal human eye level. The instinct in the human sense of sight is to tend to present anything above the normal line of vision as large and anything below that line of vision as small. For instance, a person standing on a hill in the near distance, when seen from below appears larger, whereas to the person standing above the person below appears smaller.

This is not merely a matter of looking up and looking down, however, because if you examine a printed page, although in fact the letters B and S, and the numeral 8, are larger at the bottom than at the top, we ordinarily are not conscious of it. If as a test, you invert these letters and compare the sizes, you will find that the lower part is surprisingly larger than you thought. Applying this optical illusion to the garden, we can manage the symbolizing

of hills and mountains by choosing a location that will be higher than the line of sight or by setting the stones higher than the line of sight.

This is not the same thing as lining up stones to make a small rock garden in a box or a dish to imitate the shape of mountains. In the garden, by merely setting one or two stones, we evoke the sublime force in which the atmosphere of the hills and mountains is steeped.

In the case of smaller stones or stones lower than eye level, the impression is not symbolic of the hills and mountains, but simply suggests stones in the water, on the plains, or in the mountains.

The stones F-J in row two symbolize steepness in their natural size and in their amplified sense symbolize the atmosphere of such cliffs and precipices as Japan's Mount Myogi or the rugged Teiko Ridge in China. Here again, this is not a matter of lining up a lot of stones to make a cliff-like scene, but is the setting of one stone to evoke the whole atmosphere of that type of scene. Set these stones on a high bluff's embankment, flank a waterfall with them, or combine them with the stones from row one to symbolize distant mountains and hills.

Stone K in this same row has a sharply pointed top and symbolizes bleakness and bareness. Looking at this stone does not prompt tranquility of heart. Though at first sight, such a stone seems to have an appeal, this is really only the result of the stone's affectation. A person with a healthy sense of humanity will find this stone unattractive. From ancient times, Japanese gardeners have disliked this so-called bayonet-point shape.

The stones in row three, L-P, in their natural-size atmosphere symbolize steepness, as one might expect. In their amplified atmosphere, in combination with the stones in row two, they symbolize an abyss. The stones are quite different in feeling in the case of mood symbolism, however, since the stones in row two then represent austerity, whereas the stones in row three create the impression of being at ease. These stones are most elegant when there tops are perfectly level.

Stones Q-T, in their natural size atmosphere, symbolize stability. Because in their amplified size atmosphere they create a symbol of a calm lake or some other flat quiet body of water, they are suitable for the vicinity of a pond.

In row five stones U, V, and X, in their actual size atmosphere are merely prostrate stones, but in their amplified size atmosphere they symbolize the immobility of the solid earth. Stones W,

Y, and Z, on the other hand, in their actual size atmosphere symbolize the windswept shore or the dashing and rush of rapids, because of the energetic dance-like movements of their surfaces. Because stone A′, much like stone K in row two, has sharply pointed pinnacles and suggests desolation, it fails to impart a sense of calm to the human heart, and it is safer not to use it.

Waterfalls and Rapids The activity of water in land, represented by cascades and rapids and climaxing in the waterfall, is inexhaustibly interesting and presents a variety of magnificent views from the small cascade to the tremendous falls crashing into pits and over rocks. Although usually spatial limitations in a garden make a large waterfall impractical, because there are many cases in which a cascade that symbolizes the sublime mood and the beautiful movement of the water of a waterfall plays a principle part in the mountain and water garden, we should study the construction of these cascades in as much detail as possible. It is true that if water is available in abundance you can simply let it fall over concrete without paying particular attention to stone arranging, and the falls will be beautiful. On the other hand, if water is scarce, considerable care and technical skill is needed to evoke the feeling of a waterfall. Both pleasure and perplexity accompany this process, particularly in the effort of creating a waterfall where there is no water at all. Nevertheless, in cases where there is little or no water, evoking the feeling of a waterfall means that we must remember the quiet taste, or *shibusa*, of the Japanese garden.

The three types of falls in the *Sakuteiki*, the sheet falls, the divided falls, and the so-called white thread falls, are usual found both in environments where water is abundant and where effort has to be exerted to create them. As you see in Figure 33, the sheet fall may also be a divided fall. Ordinarily the sheet fall assumes this shape, but the divided fall need not be a sheet fall; it may also be broken down into thinner falls. Figure 34 shows an example of the white thread fall. This type need not be on the grand scale of a natural white thread fall, because a fine stream, like the one in the photograph, successfully evokes the atmosphere of the real white thread fall. This fall is in the Murin-an in Nanzen-ji-machi, Kyoto.

Though these falls are in gardens that have more than the usual wealth of water, generally it is necessary to construct falls where water is scarcer. In doing this, it is essential to have the water cross over a central stone in the falls—popularly called the mirror stone —which has a concavity or a shallow V in its upper surface. Passing the water over this V cut is very important in giving the fall a dancing movement and in allowing the air to mix with the water to make the fall white. Choosing a stone with the V-shape depression is not for the purpose of deviating the water to the side. The water should pass directly over the surface of this stone.

Generally, the construction of a fall is like that shown in the basic waterfall construction chart, Figure 32. Ordinarily the fall is made up of seven stones grouped in five categories—the central stone over which the water falls, or the mirror stone, the two stones that flank the fall, and the two stones at their bases, the stone at the top of the fall over which the water passes, and the stone at the bottom of the falls which serves to divide the waves. However, it is also possible to use one stone to serve the part of two, or three to serve the part of one. In addition, in most cases, if the mirror stone projects out farther than the flanking stones on either side, the construction will not produce the proper waterfall feeling. Setting the mirror stone in as deep as possible will emphasize the gravity of the fall. Since usually the mirror stone leans back, and its lower portion may easily jut out beyond the flanking stones, set it back as much as possible for it is essential for at least the upper portions of the flanking stones to stand out resolutely. The sense of a waterfall is best produced if the flank-

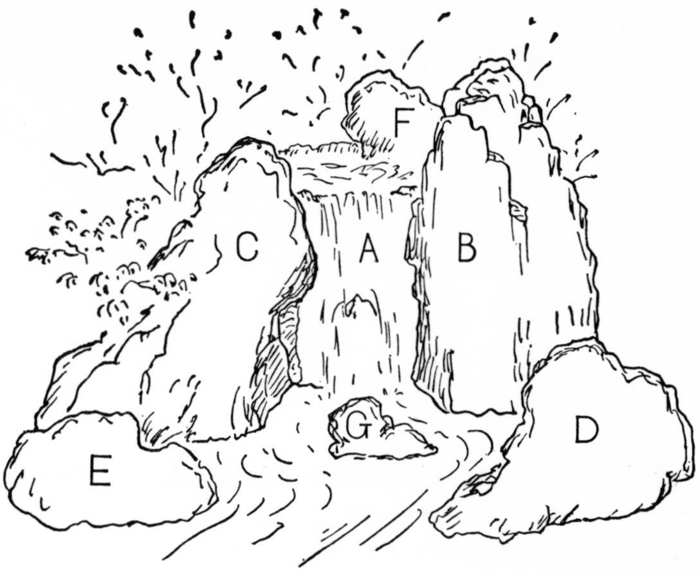

Figure 32.
Basic waterfall construction chart;
  (A) *mirror stone*
  (B *and* C) *flanking stones*
  (D *and* E) *base stones*
  (F) *water-dividing stone*
  (G) *wave-dividing stone*

ing stones stand straight, lean forward, or seem as if they are about to fall over into the cascade. It is also essential to focus the attention on the mirror stone and balance the flanking stones with it. The stone at the bottom of the fall which divides the waves should be heading into the fall. In other words, its force should be directed towards the fall so as to symbolize the force of the water. There is a stone that resembles the wave-dividing stone called the water-dividing stone, but this is used to divide the water in the fall itself when the mirror stone is actually composed of several stones. Other types of stones include a stone with which the fall water collides and a stone to cover the fall water.

Setting a shapely vertically textured stone at an angle or setting a flat stone so that it does not look level is always unsatisfactory, because such a setting results in a sense of instability. Even in stone arrangements where the grain of the stone is set at an incline if its top surface is not level, it will seem insecure.

The names mirror stone and flanking stone that we have used in the explanation of the construction of the mouth of a waterfall are names that have been in use for many years, but just as before the names came into use, so now, it is not always necessary to use these types of stones. As you see in Figure 168, showing a modern fall viewed from the Japanese-style room of Mr. F's house, it is possible to construct a water fall using only one stone.

In the dry stream garden there is absolutely no thought given to using water, but a rough textured vertical stone set like a mirror stone can create the feeling of a waterfall. Even so, using andesite slab stones like the Sendai Nebugawa stone in such cases is too arty. Particularly if the mirror stone is for water to pass over, this type of slab gives nothing of the feeling of a stone arrangement.

The mirror stone for the waterless stream, to symbolize the actual spirit of the falling water, should have a bold vertical texture pattern, which is even more effective in producing the effect of the force of water than the use of a blue or white stone would be. It is all right to choose a stone with a horizontal pattern for use in a real waterfall, but a vertical pattern in essential for the mirror stone in a waterless waterfall.

To make a waterless waterfall look like a real one it is important to make

as free use as possible of the forcefulness of the mirror stone, the flanking
and base stones, and the wave-dividing
stone. To send the water swirling and
dancing over the falls, face the water-
dividing stone at the top of the mirror
stone forcefully against the upper current. Even if one of the flanking stones
is set to stand straight and proud, one
of them should lean forward, or into
the basin of the falls. The base stones
must be set firmly so that they give a
sense of stability, but they must also
seem to be embracing the basin of the
falls. If the base stones do not have wide
spreading well set root portions, they
will not be able successfully to fulfill
their purpose. As we said before, you
may use either one wave-dividing stone,
or from three to five of them scattered
about in the fall basin, but the majority
of them should face into the current because this heightens the effect of the falling water. These water-dividing stones
are the real finishing touches of the
waterfall.

Rapids, as you can see from Figure
35, are constructed by placing stones or
some other obstacle in the stream to
restrict the water and send it dancing
along. Where the water is calm, you
may construct as many of these step-
like arrangements as you like. Because
if the water simply flows out from between the stones it will not be noticea-
ble, the rapids will be more interesting

if you send the water over the top of a
stone with a concave upper surface. If
the water is scarce, let it collect and fall
from one place, as in Figure 36, but if
it is plentiful let it fall over at a number
of points, as in Figure 35. Since if air
does not mix with the water the water
will not become white, choose a stone
with a coarse texture that will activate
the water and cause air to mix with it
as it passes over. The water will then
turn into white foam which will be conspicuous even from afar. So as not to
hide these rapids under thick vegetation, as you see in these two photographs, the garden is in a field-like style
that gleams and looks white in the light
of the sun or moon. The garden in
Figure 35 is a part of the Kyoto Murin-
an, and the dark place in the upper
center of this picture is where the white
thread waterfall in Figure 34 is.

The arrangement in Figure 37, unlike
true rapids, is not in the middle of a
stream but is the outlet from a pond.
Because the water in the pond is standing and the scenery is quiet, the stone
arrangement at the rapids is in one un-
varied straight line in keeping with the
quiet tone. In the cases of rapids in the
middle of streams the stones should be
arranged with as much variation and
as many ins and outs in the line as
possible to emphasize the flying and
dancing of the water. Figure 38 is a view
of the rapids in Figure 35 from a dif-

ferent angle and from the left bank of the stream.

Though up till this point, we have spoken of waterfalls that actually use water, Figure 39 is an example of a waterless garden in which the stone arrangement symbolizes a waterfall. This is the main section of the garden in the superior priest's quarters in the Daitoku-ji in Kyoto. The straight standing shape and the grain of the stones represent the atmosphere of a waterfall. There is a wave-dividing stone to help make the feeling of water flowing from the basin of the falls successful. The wide area of swept white sand creates the mood of a stream flowing into a lake.

Although this garden does represent the natural symbolism of which we have been speaking, if we consider the straight standing shapes and the textures of the stones as symbols of sublimity we could also view this garden as mood symbolization.

In contrast to the Kokei garden and the garden in the head priest's quarters of the Ryoan-ji, which have a dynamic beauty, this garden's beauty is tranquil.

Islands There are stones placed in the water to be nothing more than stones in the water, but there are also cases in which these stones serve to symbolize the atmosphere of islands. The stones in Figure 40 are symbols of an island. The real scene with its grasses and trees, though, is even lovelier than the picture. In addition to this type of island, it is also possible to create the atmosphere of an island with cut standing stones, stones sunk to their edges in the water so that they just break the surface, a sandbar-type island, or an island with no stone arrangement and only low reeds or mosses. Mosses are particularly lovely even in the sunlight, if there is water beneath them. Moss on a gently rising island is quiet and very natural looking. This is the so-called mountain island category which occurs frequently in lakes and marshes. Because it is not often attempted in gardens, it is interesting as a design.

Figure 33.   Sheet waterfall.

Figure 34.   White-thread waterfall.

Figure 35. Rapids in a stream.

Figure 36. Rapids used with a small supply of water.

Figure 37. Rapids at a pond outlet.

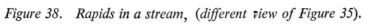

Figure 38. Rapids in a stream, (different view of Figure 35).

Figure 39.
Stone group symbolizing a waterfall,
(Daitoku-ji).

Figure 40.   Stones symbolizing an island.

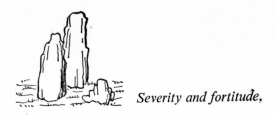

Severity and fortitude.

Peaceful stability.

D   *Mood symbolism.*

D   Mood Symbolism

Mood symbolism in the Japanese gardens came about much later than natural symbolism. An example of this type of symbolism is found in the series nobility, rashness, constancy, and calm. In the terms of the stone shape classification chart, row one and row two correspond to nobility, row three to rashness, row five to constancy, and row four to calm. Expressing this symbolism in modern terms, we could say that row one symbolizes nobility and a proper austerity which in terms of human personality would express the nature of a saint, or a wise man. Row two symbolizes manliness and severity, or the heroic personality. These stones are used a great deal in gardens where dignity is prized. The stones in row three symbolize a bouyant eccentricity which in terms of the human personality is represented by the clever, sharp man who excels in the witty. Among these stones, N, O, and P represent unrestrained extravagance, and typify the plucky, clever man. These stones serve primarily as supporting players to relieve and lighten the excessive seriousness of the stones in the first two rows, much as the commedian in the Kabuki offers comic relief to the more serious and austere characters. Use of a stone like N, however, where the pattern of the stone is too lively, would ruin the design of the arrangement and destroy its dignity. The stones in row four symbolize peace and tranquility, or the nature of a philanthropist or an affectionate mother. The stones in row five symbolize a steady vigor, though stone W represents something of the unrestrained extravagance that we saw in stones N, O, and P. In terms of personality, these stones stand for the steadfastness of a rustic. Of course, when these stones retain the same typical shapes but are small, they become more charming.

Austerity   Because there are a large number of standing stones in the Daisen-in Garden in the Daitoku-ji (*Figure 41*), the feeling is somewhat turbulent; nevertheless, the mid-Edo-period designer of the garden described his garden as austerity expressed in forms and shapes. The vertical straight textures of the stones symbolize the austerity of the stone arrangement. Although the symbolizing of distant mountains through the tall slender stones and of the nearer mountains and hills through the wide thick ones is natural symbolization, the garden's value increases because, while creating this natural symbol, it at the

Figure 41. Standing stones in the Daisen-in garden, (Daitoku-ji).

same time implies a mood symbol of austerity. In this garden the use of a number of severe shapes and grains results in a sense of severity. Had some stones inclining toward rotundity been used, a symbol of mildness would have resulted, and if a number of flat surfaced stones had been used, the resulting symbol would have been one of tranquility. Through the selection and management of the stones, a variety of different moods can be symbolized.

Vastness Figure 42 shows the sand and open-sea garden of the famous Temple of the Silver Pavilion (Ginkaku-ji). Although this is not what is usually called a stone arrangement, because the sand is raked into a startlingly different pattern, the arrangement becomes clear if we regard it as a symbol of the vastness one senses on the open sea or in the desert. In simply symbolizing sea or water scenery, flat land, or low land is desirable. In symbolizing the mood of vastness, on the other hand, the land should be elevated to emphasize the mood.

Figure 42.   Sand and open-sea garden (Ginkaku-ji).

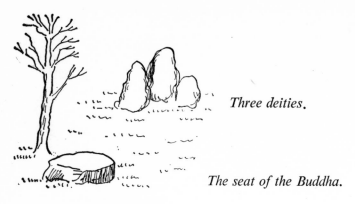

Three deities.

The seat of the Buddha.

E   Idea symbolism.

E   Idea Symbolism

Idea symbolism, unlike the more objective natural and mood symbolism, which most sensitive people can understand, is a very subjective symbolism that may not convey any meaning at all to some people whose scope may be limited to only certain ideas. For instance, one of the stones from rows one or two in the chart, standing alone might represent an object of worship, three together, might stand for the three Buddhas, or they might symbolize Mount Horaisan, or Mount Shumisen, or the famous Japanese tortoise and crane combinations. One stone from row four might represent the seat of the Buddha. Nevertheless, if the person viewing these stones has never entertained this type of idea, the idea symbolism is completely irrelevant for him. On the other hand, since these ideas are objective, arrangements expressing them are much prized in the Japanese garden by those familiar with the idea content.

Figure 43 shows the row of stones lined up to dot the pond in the Saiho-ji in Kyoto. These stones, set too far apart to be usual pond crossing stones, cannot be walked on. They are rather intended for the Arhat, the five hundred disciples of the Buddha, to cross on. This may be complete mystery to those who know nothing of Buddhism, but to the followers of the Buddhist faith these stones convey a religious idea symbol.

The stone called *Ama-no-iwafune*, or the Celestial Ship (*Figure 44*), is in the garden connected to the right side of the Daisen-in garden in the Daitoku-ji (*Figure 41*). This is not an attempt merely to set a stone in such a way that it resembles a wooden ship. From the very beginning, stones set this way have been specifically thought of as the Celestial Ship only. In Japanese mythology there is a story that, in the age of the gods, Ama-no-Sakume loaded a ship with gold, silver, and precious jewels and, sailing through space, descended to earth. This *Iwafune* is that Celestial Ship, which has become a theme of a Noh chant. The Ship of the Seven Deities, which appeared in later stories, probably also descended from this original *Iwafune*. At any rate, since it is a particularly auspicious story, these ships can probably be thought to have been made for happy gardens. The name "long ship," also applied to this arrangement, has no meaning, but is just a left-over name that was carelessly pinned to the arrangement in later years.

In the photograph, the force of this arrangement is directed to the right and has no force connection with the garden on the left because the themes of the two are clearly quite separate.

Figure 43.
Stones for the Arhat, (Saiho-ji).

Figure 44.   Celestial ship stone.

The spirit of response.

The large stone symbolizes the act of confrontal, and the small stones the act of being pursued. If these stones are set into or away from the flow of a stream they symbolize the force of the flowing water.

F   Spiritual symbolism.

F   Spiritual Symbolism

The spirit of a stone, perceived in the forceful movement of the stone's strength and power in one direction or another, is very like the feeling one gets from written calligraphy.

The arrows on each stone in the stone category chart indicate the direction in which the spirit of the stone moves. A stone set in the earth displays a spirit of being born and coming out of the earth. If there is a horn-like projection on the stone, the spirit will give the feeling of moving in the direction of that horn. When the arrow in the chart rises vertically upward, this indicates that the spirit of the stone moves vertically upward. If we construct a perpendicular to the base of a stone at the center of the base and divide the stone into sides A and B, in the cases of stones A and B, we see that the two sides have approximately the same bulk. In the case of stone C, on the other hand, since the volume of side B is greater than that of side A, the spirit of the stone moves obliquely to the right, as the arrow indicates. For the same reason, the spirit of stone D moves obliquely to the left, once again, as the arrow shows.

The spirit of stone I in row two, for the same reason, moves to the right, that of stone L in row three also to the right, but in the case of stone M, though the volumes of the two sides are about the same, the projections to right and left of the upper section result in a spirit movement to right and left. In stone N, which has several projections jutting out, the spirit moves in the various directions of the projections. The over-all average of the force of the stone is balanced. In stone O, where side A is larger than side B, the spirit of the stone runs up the incline of side A. Since in stone P there is a projection on both sides, the spirit of the stone works in both directions; nevertheless, since side B is much larger than side A the over-all spirit of the stone moves in the direction of side B. All of the stones in row four are flat and their force rather than moving to one side or another, goes straight up. All of the stones in row five are best set low, and there are only a few of them in which the spirit moves in any inclined direction. Only in W do we see this type of movement because side A is much larger than side B, causing the spirit to move in the direction of A.

In arranging stones with spirits that move in some given direction to the side or on an incline, it is essential to set them so that the respond to each other, so that they seem to pursue or flee from each other, because this gives liveliness to the arrangement. Stones whose spirits move in a directly upward direction impart a sense of stability and are very important in giving the stone arrangement an over-all feeling of composure.

In stone combinations, stones B and C in row one seem to have their backs turned. In comparison with people, they correspond to the actions of calling someone or winking to someone because the spirit of C moves in the opposite direction of that of B. They seem to be winking in the direction in which the spirit of the stone runs. Now look only at stones B, C, and D. Stones C and D seem to be winking at each other, and only B is left out. If you will look at stones O and P, you will note that they seem to be turning their backs on one another, very much like lovers who are in the brief twinkling of a difference of some sort. In any stone arrangement, to create responses among the stones and to give the feeling of connections and compactness to the arrangement, it is essential to make the spirits of the stones interexchange. Moreover, to create unity out a number of stones, all of their spirits must be gathered together in one.

The problem arises of whether a stone with a spirit that inclines to one side can be made to integrate with a vertical stone, even though their spirits' movements can be unified. Contact can be maintained between such companion stones, depending on the way they face each other. This is expressed not in the stones' spiritual forces, but in the vaguer conception of signs. In relation to humans, this is not a matter of winking, but is more the degree of feeling at which people face each other with mutual goodwill.

Because this matter of signs in stones is a more subtle sense than the spiritual forces, perhaps only those who have a deep taste for stone arranging can understand it. Nevertheless, because this is an element that accompanies spiritual symbolism in stone groups and should be considered static spiritual force, it is often found in arrangements in which straight standing stones and flat top stones are used, and if one cannot perceive this keenly, he will be unable to appreciate the mystery of the Japanese garden.

Unrestrained Extravagance Figure 45 shows the stone arrangement in the main section of the Kokei garden in the Kyoto Hongan-ji. In comparison with the Daisen-in stone arrangement, there are more stones with inclined or slanted spiritual force lines and the garden is more vigorous and seems to have made freer use of spiritual force in its theme. For this reason, the dignity of the garden suffers somewhat, but as an example of the free use of unrestrained extravagant spiritual force in stone arrangements, it is successful. The group of small stones at the left on either side of the stone bridge facing the large stone on the right are balanced, even though they retain their individuality within the group. In Figure 46 we have a view, farther to the right than that in Figure 45, of the wave-dividing stone seen at the bottom of the stone bridge. Farther inward the bases of a group of standing stones symbolizing the distant mountains and a waterfall are visible. In the inner part of the garden the tall slender standing stone that gives the feeling of the vague distance and the wide large stone and group of stones whose spiritual forces all work at angles and inclines in the foreground make this a model of the use of stones to create perspective. In trees or in stones a tall slender perpendicular shape creates a feeling of calm beauty and looks as if it were in the distance, whereas the beauty of movement and inclined forces seems to look closer. By putting the things that give a sense of distance in the distance and those that give a sense of proximity in the foreground you can achieve an effect of perspective as well as one of emphasis. The same effect will result from putting trees with fine leaves in the distance and those like the Japanese sago palm in the foreground.

"The Three Laughing in Tiger Valley" is the topic of this garden, whose design calls for a bridge where the mountain river crashes into the stones and for the three wise men Suien, Toemmei, Rikushusei on top of the bridge. The story about these three goes that one of them was seeing his friends, who lived a good way from him, off. As they were walking along they were engrossed in what they were saying when suddenly they realized that they had walked all the way to the bridge of the town of the friends from afar, and they burst out laughing. It is not enough to say only that this place has scenery that suggests the story and to give the garden this name on that basis. This garden is symbolic insofar as it represents the owner's wish to display the friendly feelings of the wise men in the tale to important guests who would be in the reception room, onto which the garden faces. It is natural symbolism because it symbolizes the atmosphere of a mountain stream without the use of water. It also contains mood symbolism of vigorous strength and a hearty spiritual symbolism.

The Demon-and-Children Rock Arrangement   In the last scroll of the *Sakuteiki*, towards the beginning, there is a passage that very skillfully expresses how the spiritual force of stones should move and interreact by explaining the nature of the demon-and-children stone arrangement. Of course, there was no particular reason to base a stone arrangement on such a theme, but it is very interesting to try to combine the spiritual forces of stones in this way. Figure 47 shows a demon-and-children stone arrangement in a portion of the roof-top garden on the Yasuda Life Insurance Building in front of the west entrance to Shinjuku Station. Demon and children is a sort of game in which some children become the demon and attempt to snatch away some other children from the opposing group. The Japanese name for the stone arrangement is *tochotocho hihikume,* the first word of which is the cry of the children who are playing the part of the demon and means, "I'll get you, I'll get you." The second part, *hihikume,* is the cry of the leader of the children who are lined up opposed to the demon.

The child that the demon must catch is at the rear of the line of children. In the front of this line, the leader boastfully confronts the demon and spreads his arms wide to protect the other children. As the demon runs to the right to get the child in the rear, the leader also moves to the right causing the line of children to swing to the left, so that the demon cannot come close. All of the children in the line hang on to the sashes of the children in front of them, and they all move from side to side as the demon moves. It is expressing this movement that makes the active beauty of the stone arrangement interesting.

In Figure 47, the three-stone group on the left represents the demon, the large stone on the right represents the leader of the children, and the smaller stones strung out in the rear represent the line of children. In the arrangement there are actually more small stones on the right than are shown in the photograph. The force of the stone on the left works to the right, and the force of the stone on the right responds by working to the left. The two groups confront each other so as to present no opportunities for a break through. The small stones behind the leader stone are all set so as to seem as if they were running after the leader. In this case it is important, for the sake of the liveliness of the arrangement, to avoid setting three stones in a straight line because doing so tends to dull the activity of the setting. The low flat stone in the center foreground was put there because this space was too empty and because with its quiet beauty it seems to be watching the more active beauty of the other stone arrangement. Incidental-the other stone arrangement. The raked Shirakawa sand is arranged well in that the pattern is parallel with the lines of the building except where the stones are sunk into it.

Figure 45. *Free and forceful stone arrangement* (*Kyoto Hongan-ji*).

Figure 46. *Stones creating a sense of perspective* (*Kyoto Hongan-ji*).

Figure 47. A particularly successful and charming demon-and-children stone arrangement.

Gradually climbing to a crescendo.

Melodic spacing.
The open area at A gives life to the melodic
arrangement.

G   Melodic symbolism.

G   Melodic Symbolism

Just as in music, in stone arrangements too there are highs and lows, strong places and weak places. If these highs and lows, strongs and weaks are controlled, the person who views the arrangement will be reminded of the rhythm of music. In the stone category chart (*Figure 31*) the stones in row two correspond to musical highs, the stones in row one with mid-ranges in music, that is, the tall stones represent the highs, the low stones the lows, the large stones the strength, and the small stones the weaker places. If the stones are combined to form breaks and graduations, the whole arrangement will progress to a climax.

Though we divide the symbolism of stone arrangements into five major divisions, this does not mean that one stone arrangement will represent only one type of symbolism. Instances in which a stone group combines, say, natural symbolism with any number of the other types of symbolism are plentiful.

Gradual crescendo   In Figure 48 we see a sea-wall made of rubble arranged in a random pattern. This is not unusual, but in this case, there was the question of how to preserve the interesting and subdued tastes of the scars left by the materials' former use. Be-

cause arranging the flat-topped cylinders in varying standing heights to give the feeling of crescendo is interesting, and since large cylinders of diameters of over 40 inches could be arranged in this stairstep fashion in such a large garden, the result is splendid. However, these cylinders represent a particular taste. It would be more usual to use either this type of rubble or natural hexagonal stones from Kamishima in the Izu Islands.

In the case of thick and slender stones, the thick stones should be set high. If you are using rubble, because the thick stones are often short, set them high and cover their bases with other stones in the front. When arranging stones in long continuous standing lines create variations in height within a line and, at the same time, when you have set a line of stones, create crescendos in height with the lines of stones that are to be in front and behind the first one set. Flat round stones should be controlled in size and height to bring life to the over-all arrangement.

Climax   Figure 49 shows only the principle part of the garden of the Sampo-in in Kyoto. The stone standing in the center is the famous Fujito stone, which is flanked to the right and the left in a design called the *hin* shape, because it resembles the Chinese character *pin*. This character consists of three small squares arranged in two rows, one in the center on the top. Though the flat stones are set to face the standing stone and look out over the pond, they are a very vital point in the stone arrangement because they set off the standing stone to such good advantage. There is a contrast between this line and the side line, and the gentle horizontality of these flat stones softens the strength of the standing stone.

We do not know whether the main stone is called the Fujito stone because it was brought from the Fujito Rapids or because it is connected with the Noh chant dealing with Fujito, but we believe that it has some direct connection with the chant.

People who see this stone are sure to find it impressive and appealing. It is located near the water and conceals within the severity of its shape something of a symbol of the hero of the Fujito Noh chant.

There are many stones in this garden, but it would be nearly impossible to point out any that are unnecessary. The gradual crescendo of the number and of the heights of the stones leads to the climax of the garden, the Fujito stone. Anyone who sees this garden will understand the true garden mastery of the Yoshiro brothers, Sen and Kentei, who created it. On the other hand, in the photograph of the small stones placed in front of large stone (*Figure 50*) there would be no objection to removing all of the small stones except the whiteish one on the right and lowering the base of the large stone so that it seemed to come directly up out of the water. In such a case it would also be good to remove the small stones from the front of the large stone on the left and lower that it also. The treatment of the separated large stone, which rises from the water on the right side of the Fujito stone, is more polished than this.

Figure 48.   Cylindrical stones forming a crescendo.

Figure 49.   The famous Fujito *stone, the climax of the Sampo-in garden.*

Figure 50.   Small stones grouped in front of large stones (Sampo-in garden).

Proportion through antagonism. The chart showing response in stone arrangements is another example of this type.

Proportion through disagreement. If stone A were not in the group the proportion would be lost unless there were another stone where there is a circle of dotted lines.

Precedence. The stones on either side are subordinate to the main stone in the center.

H Stone arrangement precedence and proportion.

H Proportion and Precedence in Stone Arrangements

In addition to the various formal types of beauty and the spatial constructions one must create in stone groups with various contents, proportion and precedence are also very important.

When we constructed a perpendicular from the base of stone A in the stone shape category chart and divided the stone into sides A and B, we saw that these two sides were almost the same and that they were symmetrical. In a similar manner, we can see symmetry in such stones as B, E, F, G, H, M, Q, and others where the sides are equal. Stones C and D are not symmetrically arranged since A is less than B in one case, and A is greater than B in the other. They are stable, however, because they are balanced. In stone N, the sides are equal, but since the right is vastly different from the left the two parts cannot be called symmetrical. They do, nevertheless, give a sense of balance. In stone O, where A is greater than B, and in stone P, where A is less than B, though the volumes of the sides are radically different the stones are stable and balanced and do not seem at all to be about to fall over. If we were to think of putting stones O and P together in one stone arrangement, even though O is less than P and P's volume is greater, the stones would seem to balance. In this way, even in the case of a large number of stones, if the stones balance, the entire arrangement will be stable from the beginning.

In Figure 51 we see the left corner of the garden in the head priest's quarters of the Ryoan-ji. In this case a small stone is subordinated to a large stone to form a coherent arrangement that displays the unity of the so-called beauty of precedence. A coherent stone group will result even in cases where the stones are not proportional and are arranged in opposition to each other if the weak stone is subordinated to the stronger one. It would not be an exaggeration to say that almost all Japanese garden stone groups are made coherent through this type of formal beauty of precedence and proportion.

The picture of the stone at the entrance to the rock garden in the Ryoan-ji was taken from almost the center of the head priest's main room. Since the spirit of the large stone works to the right, there had to be something on the right to respond to it, much as there must be someone to respond to anyone who called out in a loud voice. The things that are being called are the standing stone in the center and the prostrate stone in the foreground of Figure 52, in which we see the garden from the front-most corner. Figure 53 shows the stone arrangements on the left side of the Ryoan-ji garden as seen from the entrance. The spirit of the large stone there seems, from this vantage point, to be working to the left, or in the opposite direction. This is simply because of the small prop stone on the left side of the large stone which gives the large stone the feeling of responding to the stones in the inner section of the garden. If we were to take away the smaller prop stone, the large stone would lose its connection with the other stones in the garden, and the balance of the garden would dissolve to nothing. However, if the spirit of the stone worked to the right when seen from the entrance, as it does when seen from the priest's quarters (*Figure 51*), neither the absence nor the presence of the prop stone would be of any consequence.

Figure 54 is an over-all chart of the Ryoan-ji garden as seen from the central part of the priest's quarters. Judging from only the picture of the left stone group (*Figure 53*) there seems to be not even a spiritual connection between the large stone in the left foreground and the two small stones in the inner right portion of the garden. If you compare Figures 51 and 52, you will see that the large stone in Figure 51 is figuratively pursuing the two small stones in the inner left of Figure 52. The large standing stone in the center of Figure 52 acts as a screen to protect the two small stones behind it, while the large stone on the left glowers at them. Although this standing stone seems to be reticently protecting the little stones as a quiet straight standing stone when it is seen from the central portion of the priest's quarters, if it is viewed from the right of the priests quarters it gives the feeling of the energy of someone's calling out something like, "Hey, wait there!" because one part of it projects to the left causing the spirit of the stone to work to the left. The spirit of an entire stone arrangement points up the proportions of the volumes of the various stones and the energy of the movement. This, in turn, gives rise to a sense of balanced energy and precedence and a recognition of the arrangement's beauty. In this garden the principal role is played by the standing stone in the center of the entire arrangement, but since this stone is too small to be a leader and is smaller than the large stone in the left corner, the spatial construction has been arranged essentially for balance between these two stones. This is something like a symbolic emperor in a democratic country.

The popular name for this arrangement, "Delivering over the Tiger's Cubs," very aptly expresses the spiritual movement of the garden. The tiger's young cubs are represented by the small two-rock group in the upper right, the tigress by the standing stone in the center, and a leopard by the large stone on the left. The remaining stones are the other small and large offspring of the tiger. The movement of the arrangement is very well expressed if the standing stone is taken as the mother tigress confronting the leopard in the corner, while the cubs hide behind their mother's back. The interest of this arrangement lies in the free use of vigorous movement to portray the pursual and flight of the stones. In this sense, this is a particularly successful work and one that must be preserved.

Figure 51 (above).
Large stone in the left corner of the Ryoan-ji garden.

Figure 52 (right).
Ryoan-ji garden seen from far right corner.

Figure 53 (below).
Left corner seen from entrance to the Ryoan-ji garden.

Figure 54 (below right).
An over-all sketch of the Ryoan-ji garden.

§4 Planting

A Refinement in Planting

Even an ordinary sunny residential garden can become a plaintive light garden or an elegant garden if we plant in it the same kinds of refined mountain and field flowers used in the ancient tree and flower gardens or make it into an open lawn with a feeling of the field edges and paths that were also a part of some ancient Japanese gardens. For this reason, one of the essentials in creating a refined garden is to avoid the gorgeous flowering plants and to choose shrubs and grasses that flower white, pale lavender, or greenish white. Also wind-pollinated plants are preferable. Some evergreens to use are the pasania, Arabian jasmin, *tabu*, bayberry, *hisakagi*, *asebo*, *kuroganemochi*, Chinese black pine, Japanese red pine, or black pine, all of which are refined types. You might also use deciduous trees such as *konara*, *soro*, *shidezakura*, *daimyo* oak, *gonzui*, *nanakamado*, Japanese horse-chestnut, varieties of the maple, *dodan*, winter sweet, witchhazel, and finetooth holly. Some of the beautiful tasteful flowers of the cherries, for instance, *akame-yamazakura* and the quietly tasteful Japanese apricot also belong to this group of refined plants.

If the garden is not at your usual place of residence and you are not too worried about an abundance of sunlight, a half-shaded place is a suitable environment for a tasteful, refined garden. For instance, the camellia in the shade does not bloom with such gorgeous beauty as it does in the sunlight. It is also essential to have a place where it is easy to raise mosses. Be cautious of shady places, though they are good, because, if too dark, they become gloomy and dark and overdo the *shibusa*.

There are instances in which something showy can be refined and its beauty emphasized by planting. For instance, a spacious magnificent building, a crag, a tower, a stone lantern, a piece of sculpture, a waterfall, an expanse of water, or any other eye-catching object if now hidden, now revealed, by foliage will become more gracefully composed, and near things will seem to recede into the distance. You can conceal a part of an object with dense foliage and let the main part, or at least one part, be visible through the sparser leaves. In applying this method, in the first case the trees should be planted contiguous with the object to be concealed, and in the second case the object should be farther away and the trees planted immediately in front of the eyes of the viewer. Planting techniques are much the same in most of the countries of the world, and I intend to deal here only with those facets of planting that are most typically Japanese.

B Elegant Planting

To create a sense of elegance, the plants with elegant leaf shapes like the bamboo and the *kakuremino* are often used.

Figure 56 is an example of this type of planting where the elegance of the shape of the *kakuremino* leaves and its slender stalks is emphasized as they seem to float against the background of the wall. In spaces like this one, close up against a wall, where there is not much sunlight, plants like the *kakuremino* that require little light are just right.

Another type of elegant planting is seen in Figure 55 where the soft and graceful foliage of *kan* bamboo is backed by a wall and some lattice work. Any such bamboo as arrow bamboo, daimyo bamboo, *shiho* bamboo, *taimin* bamboo, or *narihira* bamboo would also be suitable. The use of a plant like the *moso* bamboo results in a feeling more of mystery than of elegance and tends to darken the refinement of the garden.

The various types of cryptomeria cedar also result in a similar darkening of the refinement. In Figure 57 there is a cryptomeria planted beside the doorway of a house to create some of this sense of darkened refinement. Planting *asebo* (*Figure 58*) in its natural shape around the base of the cryptomeria would be better than planting something like rounded azaleas, because rounded shapes do not harmonize with the feeling of this tree.

C. Vignetting a Building

In Figure 59 we see an example of pruning to surround a porch. This resembles the foundation planting method, but in this case, framing the lines of the porch creates a refined atmosphere and strengthens the connection between the house and the garden. This same method could be used in the front garden of a concrete building so that the gentleness of the greenery could soften the magnificence of the building and make for a more refined, more comfortable, feeling.

Figure 55.   Bamboo and lattice.

Figure 56.   Planting against a wall.

Figure 57.   Cryptomeria by a doorway.

Figure 58.   Cryptomeria and azaleas.

Figure 59. Pruning to surround a porch.

D Contrasts in Planting

Although introducing any type of plant with branches at different angles or with different leaf sizes into a uniformly planted setting will add a note of contrast and make the two types of plants mutually set each other off to a good advantage, using sharply pointed, straight-standing conifers among rounded evergreens or deciduous trees creates a particularly lovely contrast. In Figure 60 we see a picture of a portion of the Koki-an garden in which all of the plants and trees seem of about the some sort, but in Figure 61 there is another view of the same garden in which the addition of *momi* firs towering into the sky seems, by contrast, to open our eyes to the beauty of the entire landscape planting. In the same way, a deciduous tree planted among evergreens will also give the same effect of contrast. In a uniform setting of either evergreens or deciduous trees, a tree like the zelkova or the gingko which rise carefree and spread tall at the top, or a tree whose leaves turn red planted among some evergreens, are examples of this type of contrast planting. In the Koki-an garden, there is a thatched arbor with a stream behind it. There are no stone arrangements or clipped shrubs in sight, only the naturally luxuriant grove and lawn by the gurgling shallow stream. In Figure 61 you will notice that the stones used are all very low. This garden has a completely different sense from those that feature the spirit of undulations and grains of stones. The better Meiji gardeners used this type of method in their greatest works. For a gardener who used low stones, this one can easily be considered among the best. This garden certainly represents an advance, in that various elements of mystery are grasped and the feeling of refinement is maintained by avoiding obvious expression. It is possible to excessively and willfully make use of the spirits of standing stones or stone grains, but to avoid losing the quiet taste of the garden a great deal of refinement is necessary. Regardless of how mediocre the stone, if you set it so that its face seems turned slightly away in another direction, you will be correct. Japanese garden stone arrangements reached maturity after long experience in correct stone displaying.

Figure 60. Plants of uniform shape in the Koki-an garden.

Figure 61. Momi *fir contrasting with other plants in the Koki-an garden.*

Figure 62.   Garden walk at the Nishiyama villa.

E   Blending with the Background

Figure 62 shows a walk in a portion of the garden of the Nishiyama Villa where Tokugawa Mitsukuni lived and enjoyed himself in retirement in Ibaragi Prefecture. The portion of the garden in the photograph is simple and was apparently restored in the Tempo era (1830–1843) by Zaisho. The building in Figure 63, which shows the Nishiyama Villa Japanese apricot in the foreground, is a *shoin*-style building built by Zaisho. The pattern of the garden in this area suits the building and is composed of placements of hills and trees. It can well be thought to be a product of its age.

As one can see from the picture, there are almost none of those stones that might be called scenic in this garden. The atmosphere is that of a field with gently undulating lawns. The natural grove is the background against which a number of old Japanese apricots stand; however, these apricot trees, by seeming to be a continuation of the natural grove and by forming a connecting link with it, maintain the feeling of natural vegetation and give a sense of the limitlessness of Nature to the confined garden. This villa garden, which consists of only plants and no stone groupings at all, is a brilliant work which is yet a step ahead of the preceding example, where low stones were employed. Although there are some plain stones used at the mouth of the waterfall, which is not seen in the photograph, these stones have almost no connection with the real value of the garden.

F   Perspective Emphasis

In Figure 64, we see an example of how viewing the middle ground and distant ground of the garden through the trees planted in the foreground heightens the sense of perspective. In this case trees with no lower branches were planted near the house, and the middle ground of the garden is clearly seen through them. This type of planting is also pleasant to encounter during a leisurely walk around the house.

Figure 63. Shoin *building with Japanese apricot.*

Figure 64. *Heightening the sense of perspective.*

G Contrasts between Pruning and Natural Planting

In Figure 65 there is a good deal of rounded pruning work to contrast with the natural forest in the background. In addition, so that the forest and the garden will not come into direct contact, there is a straight-line hedge partition which makes the garden symbolize brightness. If the hedge were an earthen or plank fence, it would give a sense of crudeness to the stone arrangement and would reduce the merits of the garden by half. Moreover, if the boundary were made of naturally planted shrubs, the garden would be gloomy, its brightness would diminish, and the contrast between it and the natural grove would be lost.

There are a large number of flat-topped broad stones in this stone arrangement which give a feeling of composure. To prevent the two large stones seeming to be submerged directly in the water, small stones are grouped in front of them. Although these small stones are an eyesore, they are primarily the result of the garden designer's taste. Ordinarily, the stones are made to look as if they come into direct contact with the water, and if small stones are necessary, they are set separately.

The pruned shrubs behind the large stones are all three too much of a level. Lowering the center part would have resulted in a rhythmic feeling.

Figure 66 is a continuation of the same scene in Figure 65. The grotesque stone on the other side of the bridge destroys the graceful atmosphere of the dragon-fly lantern and the quietness of the other stone groups. It is thought that this stone was set in the garden because it resembled the helmet of Lord Kato Kiyomasa, a famous Japanese *samurai* of olden times, with whom the garden has some connection. Nevertheless, the stone looks something like a drunkard who has staggered into the company of a group of well-behaved gentlemen. In the case of humans, this drunkard would be on the verge of being removed from the group, but here he merely boasts and brags as if he were the master of the house.

If the water is clear such a stone is fine, but if the water lilies spread about too thickly, it seems that the drunkard has gotten out of hand and is throwing small pots about. (A few water lilies on the broad surface of a pond look more beautiful than too many.)

Because this stone is too strong and overpowering, it would be more in keeping with the personality of Lord Kato, who donated the quiet lantern, if it were moved farther into the interior of the garden and were made more tasteful by some of the so-called garden mystery. Say what we will, however, the designer of this garden was very talented, and it is only natural that the garden with its gracefully beautiful stone arrangements, controlled through pruning, and its ample contrasts with the background, should be famous and highly regarded.

In Figure 67, in the azaleas planted at the base of the pine, we see an instance in which pruning, though round pruning, became unconsciously over extended and caused the design to run wild. On the right side of the pine, where there are low boughs, it would be just as well to have nothing planted at the base at all. If there is to be base planting, the plants should be about one half the height of the ones we see in the picture to suit the design. Anyone who sees the lower branches of the pine and the planting under it will be struck with a sense of gloom. The over-all balance would have been better if there had been two pruned plants on the left side. It is important in trimming to be careful of the proper heights and sizes of the plants, because it is not good if the plants planted at the base of a stone to set the stone off actually conceal the stone or if they project into the important tree branches above.

Just as I have never heard of Beethoven's allowing one section of a score to run wild for the sake of the growth of another, in gardening, letting a section run wild for the growth of another part of the garden is evidence of negligence.

Figure 65.   *Rounded pruning with a natural forest.*

Figure 66.   *Rounded pruning with an island and a bridge.*

Figure 67.   Round pruning that has gotten out of control.

Figure 68.
Pruned bamboo grass.

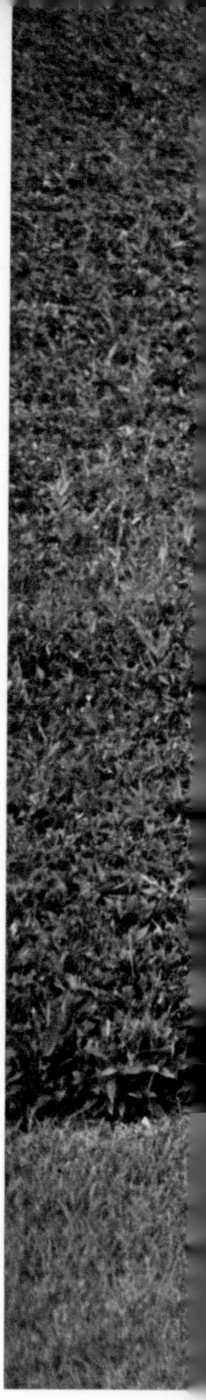

H   Pruning to Symbolize Mountains

Figure 68, showing bamboo grass pruned to resemble mountains, is a scene at the Koishikawa Korakuen garden in Tokyo. The bamboo grasses in their natural shape grow in soft thick clumps and are inherently elegant. Sometimes, however, the beauty of the pruned shape is needed for a design.

I   Applications of Pruning

Ordinarily we prune hedges, plants for the bases of stones, and plants that represent actual mountains, buildings, or animals. Since there is quite a margin in what can be done with pruning, the future will probably see the development of many fresh designs, which will not be limited to some sort of mood symbols or abstractions but will be a field for real creative originality.

In terms of current pruning, as you see in Figure 69, pruned shrubbery is used behind stone arrangements in place of a hedge. If pruning is based on the rectangle in combination with proper straight standing stones it gives a sense of orderliness. On the other hand, if there is some complicated pruning work behind stones, it makes the stones stand out clearly in a theatrical effect. In such an instance, rather than mix the shrubbery with a hedge, use a single type of plant for a better effect. This type of backing, rather than an earthen wall or a plank fence, is valuable for the variety it gives as the seasons change.

Figure 69.
Rectangular pruning and
standing stone.

117

§5 *Various Middle Ground Arrangements*

A   The Garden Path

Though for a garden path in a private residence 20–24 inches is a suitable width, in a place where there is much coming and going, such as an inn or any other public building, paths might be two or four yards wide. In Figure 70 the path with the stake fence will permit two people to walk abreast. A stake fence with holes in the wood for rope to pass through is a pleasant and relaxing type. In Figure 71, which is the other side of the scene in Figure 70, the standing stone in the arrangement at the bottom of the shrubbery seems to be merely a small stone perched there, because the prostrate stones nearby are taller and seems to overpower the standing stone. Balance is best achieved in this type of arrangement if the prostrate stones are set low by burying them half in the ground.

In Figure 72, we see a staircase of natural stone, set into an inclined garden path. These stones, which are natural stones rather than ordinary stepping stones, harmonize perfectly with the setting.

The staircase in Figure 73 is made of logs laid sideways on a gentle incline and, like the preceding figure, is very tasteful and blends well with its surroundings because there are no high stones around the path.

Figure 70. Garden fence and stake fence.

Figure 71. Faulty height balance in standing stones.

Figure 73. Log staircase.

119

Figure 72. Natural-stone staircase.

B The Bridge

A bridge should be built in a garden at only the place where one is inevitable. There is a sequestered stone bridge (*Figure 74*) in the Ryoan-ji gardens, which, is an example of a garden bridge, that is particularly inevitable. In places where the water level is low and the trees around it are dark and luxuriant, an old-looking somber stone bridge will suit. In such cases, a bridge of natural stones arranged in a tortoise shell pattern will emphasize the lowness of the water and will give a sense of repose. Piling up cobble stones gradually will make the water level seem higher, but in such cases, making the bridge low will evoke a feeling of intimacy with the water. This is the only arrangement to show this type of calm repose.

In Figure 75, in the central right section of the picture is a low stone bridge which is a part of the garden of the Ninna-ji. Because this is not a particularly secluded garden, making the bridge low creates a feeling of intimacy with the stream. The bench built out into the garden from one section of the veranda is interesting. Since this bench juts out into the area over the garden, it seems to project into the greenery and to form a connection between the building and the garden.

The high bridge in Figure 76 is in a part of the Koki-an Gardens. It is suitably arched high over a mountain stream, on both banks of which trees grow thick enough to hide the stones. In the bottom of the little canyon are bamboo grass, Japanese aucuba, and Japanese aralia. Because the bridge is high the arch is suitable, but if the bridge had been lower an earthen bridge or a log bridge would have been better. When the bridge was built the stones probably looked like mountains, but this rustic and quiet scene doubtless developed as the grasses and trees became thicker and more luxuriant. Figure 77 shows a neck of a pond with a bridge in the Daigo-sampo-in Gardens. This bridge is built at a very logical inevitable place where two peninsulas jut out from either bank to form a very narrow neck in the pond. Although in front of the bridge there are stones that actually seem to be about to fall into the pond, from the aspect of the pond shown in the photograph, these stones seem insecure. In so far as the tops of the stones are flat, they look better set to the right. However, if we shift our angle and view them from farther right, the stone tops average out in both directions and seem stable. The stone that is set to butt into the bridge at its approach is necessary to give a sense of calm.

The bridge made of joined boulders, in Figure 78, is in a garden in a recently completed mountain villa. The heavily grained stones give the feeling of the gardens of old. The stones on the far side of the bridge that have horizontal graining are graceful because they are very well set. Since the bridge is brand new, a large quantity of sweet rush or ferns should be planted in the cracks between the stone to create a sense of calm.

The zigzag bridge in Figure 79 is only one type of a widely used bridge construction method. These bridges are made of the halved logs of such trees as pasania or the chestnut with the flat tops up. Charred cryptomeria logs arranged in this pattern are also good. Zigzag bridges are always built not too high from the surface of the water or from the level of a dry stream so as to give a feeling of easy intimacy.

The zigzag bridge in Figure 80, which is made of flat lumber, would be even nicer if it were four inches lower. It is also better to use low stones in a number of levels at either end of the bridge so that they seem to descend towards the bridge. In this instance the supports of the bridge extend about the width of the bridge up from the bridge surface. This is fine, but if they seem too tall, they may also be easily altered to one half or to two thirds the width of the bridge. We can see that the man who made this bridge took great care with beauty of proportion.

The next two figures are of bridges in two of Japan's most outstanding gardens: the gardens of the Sendo Palace and the gardens of the Katsura Detached Palace. It is unjustifiable to build a low bridge that is also useful in a place where there should be a high bridge, and if it is to be high, a stone bridge with a bent handrail is suitable. Nevertheless, dressing up the top section like an upper bridge is artificial. In the photograph of the Sendo Palace bridge (*Figure 81*), however, we don't seem to notice this failing and the bridge is pleasing. This may be for a variety of reasons. Perhaps it is because the legs of the bridge are tall and we can sense the composure of the water beneath. Perhaps the gravity of the over-all shape of the bridge is impressive. Perhaps the tall trees around the shore keep the excess height of the bridge from being discordant. A strong point of this garden is the gently sloping stone beach that descends into the water itself.

Although the bridge at the Katsura Detached Palace (*Figure 82*) is not tall enough to give a sense of the serenity of the water, its lack of height evokes a feeling of the vastness of water. The long broad stone at the approach is certainly inimitable. Though it is tall and slender, as might be expected, the use of a stone that is not sharply pointed is important.

Figure 74. Stone bridge in the Ryoan-ji.

Figure 75. Low stone bridge seen from the veranda of the Ninna-ji.

Figure 76. Arched high bridge made of a single stone.

Figure 77. Bridge between pond promontories (Daigo sampo-in garden).

Figure 78.   Bridge of joined boulders.

Figure 79. Zigzag bridge.

Figure 80. Flat lumber zigzag bridge.

Figure 81. *Bridge at the Sendo Palace.*

Figure 82.   Bridge in the Katsura Detached Palace garden.

C Stepping Stones for a Pond or Stream

Although perhaps the arrangement of stepping stones in combination with a bridge in Figure 83 is a little dangerous for night walking, the design is certainly interesting. The concavity and convexity of the sides of the flat stones is skillfully combined with the round stone piles to result in a completely unforced feeling. Instead of using a stone like those used at the approaches to ordinary bridges, here the designer chose to enclose the corners of the flat stones in groups of clinging smaller stones.

In Figure 84 we see an example of stones in a brook where the flowing and rippling of the abundant water is itself a sufficiently beautiful sight. The stepping stones that form a row on the left side of the stream are not at all conspicuous, and as you can see from the photograph they are dispensable. Nevertheless, they were probably set as they are because of some need. Variation has been provided by arranging, here and there, a large natural stone so that it can be walked over and by then using smaller stones in groups for passage. The stones in the middle of the stream are left sprinkled about naturally with no decorative features and no sense of motif.

In Figure 85 there are stepping stones across a dry stone beach. These are, of course, not in a pond or in a stream,

but they suggest a future inundation when these mere stepping stones will become stones in a stream. The stones that make up the beach are set very much like paving stones. In an ancient book on gardening there is a statement to the effect that one must not set stepping stones in a stone beach, neither must he allow moss to grow there. This means that since the gravel in a stone beach arrangement is easy to move, the spirit of a beach will vanish if stepping stones are neatly set in it. On the other hand, stepping stones set here and there so that one can pick one's way across the beach will not destroy the mood. The mention of not allowing moss to grow on the stones refers to cases in which one evokes the feeling of a seaside beach. If the stone beach of a mountain stream is the aim of the arrangement, moss may be used.

The round mill stones in Figure 86 are set in the pond in the garden of the Heian Shrine in Kyoto. In this instance nothing but these mortar-like round stones has been used. This is a case in which the pleasure of viewing the stones is more important than the pleasure of walking across them. Since no labour is needed to set round stones so that the blend together, they can be freely varied in something resembling a line of birds or in the flight pattern of geese. These round stones have come to characterize this particular garden and attract much public attention.

Figure 83.
Bridge with stepping
stones.

Figure 84. Stepping stones in a rippling brook.

Figure 85.   Stepping stones on a stone beach.

Figure 86.   Round stepping stones at the Heian Shrine.

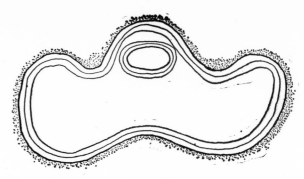

Shin shape

D The Shape of the Pond and its Banks

From ancient times ponds in Japanese gardens have employed such designs as the irregular shape of the character *shin*, which means heart, the cloud shape, or the bottlegourd shape, but since the shape of the pond depends primarily on the shape of the plot of land, cases in which the shape of the pond can be chosen from the very beginning are rare. If a varied shape is your main aim, you will probably want to have promontories jutting out alternately from the right and left. The *shin* shape, the cloud shape, and the bottle-gourd shape are all suitable to that type of pond. If the pond is to be viewed from only one side, it is often better to have a section within the promontories on either side that is narrower than the front water surface. If you want the feeling of the bright full waters of spring, have the surface of the water high enough and close enough to the banks so that the ponds seems to be in a flood state. If you want to be able to look down from between the trees to a calmer scene, a water level lower than the banks is effective. On banks that are close to the surface of the water it is good to plant grasses that seem to touch the pond. If the bank is farther away from the surface of the water straight vertical stones or boulders that lean out over the water are suitable. Sand or

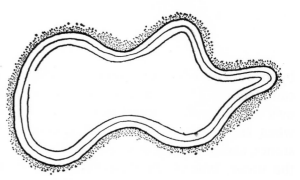

cloud shape

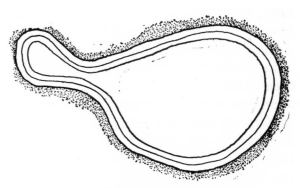

bottle-gourd shape

small round stones leading in a gently inclined line to, and continuing into the water are also interesting. However, if you use sand, it is necessary to place some small round stones at the edge of the water to keep the sand from washing away.

Straight standing trees and low shrubbery are suitable for a grass or lawn bank, whereas if there is a stone cliff nearby, trees with long boughs that lean out over the water and cast their reflection into the pond so that the surface of the water is now seen and now hidden by the foliage will give a composed and calm feeling. Trees that cast their shadows on the water should not be used when there are cobbles, small round stones, sand, or grass that continue into the water, because in these cases it is best to be able to have an unobstructed view of the reflections of the sky and clouds on the pond surface. Use a freely curving shore line for ponds with a grass, sand, or pebble beach, and a violently indented shore line for a cliff shore for natural strength.

In comparing the shore line and the area of the pond, we can say that if the shoreline is made comparatively more important, emphasis is on variation in the shape of the pond and its surroundings, whereas if the opposite is the case, the important aim will be to reflect the sky, clouds, distant mountains, or some other scenic feature.

A pond with straight stone banks should be arranged in a straight line or in a curve, as you see in Figures 87 and 88. The banks of a pond with natural pebbles should look like the pond in Figure 89. Banks like those of a river with small stones or a beach-type arrangement where the edges might crumble into the water should be planted with small bamboo grasses or rushes at the edge. There are a number of other types, but essentially the banks of a pond are to contain the water where there is no distant underground water or natural springs and to prevent the erosion of the ground at the banks. In pond scenes like those in Figure 167 (*See page 231*) of Mr. F's pond for a Japanese-style room or Mr. N's pond in Figure 156, the bottoms and the sides of the ponds are made of concrete and finished in mortar concealed by a stone arrangement and a line of round stones at the edge. This was done more to prevent the water from seeping away than to keep the earth from collapsing. It also enhances the scene and matches the imposing exteriors of the buildings.

The straight-shore-style pond in Figure 87 is in a section of the gardens of the Katsura Detached Palace. The stone lantern in the upper right of the photograph is an example of the *Sanko* style. Because the lantern is small, it seems to be very far away and makes the pond look much more spacious. From the other side of the pond the lantern can be seen reflected in the water.

The straight bank pond in Figure 88 shows an example of stepping stones descending gradually to the edge of the pond. The stone lantern, when seen from above, seems to have the surface of the water as a background. It is particularly lovely when lighted because its reflection in the water can be seen from the opposite bank. In Figure 89 we see natural small stones surrounding a muted large stone on a pleasant lawn that slopes gently to the edge of the pond. If the slope had been even more leisurely than this and had continued to the water the mood would have been more relaxed, and the pond, the lawn, and all the surroundings would be more comfortable. In Figure 90, although stones have been used in generous curves in the shoreline, they are set low and the lawn and shrubbery of the slope continue to the water line which fluctuates very little. Merely lining the stones up this way has the effect of making the surface of the water seem more spacious.

In Figure 91 we see a graceful pond where the stones on the edge have been set low to be inconspicuous. The central island contains large stones, which are well set and have flat tops so that they are not flashy. In old gardens, where the shrubbery has flourished, the feeling is one of calm relaxation and the weak points in the stone settings are concealed. Because all of the base plants are pruned round, a graceful openness takes the place of a feeling of naturalness.

We might say that the principle sym-bolism of this garden is of a mood of graceful charm. In this type of garden it is essential to the maintaining of the beauty of the scene to keep the lawn paths closely trimmed. Though this might seem troublesome, putting stones between the lawn and the paths would destroy the appearance of the garden.

In the upper portion of the photograph in Figure 92, which shows a shoreline made up of stones with striking grains, the legs of the people constructing the garden are visible. The stones themselves still look naked because the gardeners have yet to set plants around their bases. The stones are too open and fail to give a pleasing feeling because their grains are prominent, and they seem gloomy. Although stones large in proportion to the size of the pond may be used in making the bank, to save them from excess variations and fluctuations plant base plants around them or cover them in moss, and they will do quite well. When the stones in this picture are about half hidden in plants, the garden will be finished.

Figure 87. Straight shore of pond at the Katsura Detached Palace.

Figure 88. Stepping stones to a straight pond shore.

Figure 89. Natural pond edge of small stones.

Figure 90. Gently curving shore.

Figure 91. Pond with edging stones and island.

Figure 92. Unfinished pond with conspicuous stone textures.

E   The Dock

This is a place where boats may come in if the pond is large, or where one may go to rinse one's hands or to feed the fish if the pond is small. At any rate it is a place of intimacy with the water where one feels he can go and reach out and touch the pond's surface. For this reason the dock should be close to the surface of the pond, should jut out into the pond to emphasize the mood of closeness to the water. From the level of the water the dock should be no higher than four-eight inches, because if it is as high as twelve inches, the platform will be to far from the water.

The dock in Figure 93 consists of a platform made of one large thin stone. Rather than have the stone rise straight from the water like a column, a wide space is emptied out at the bottom of the stone so that the platform seems to float out over the water. Had the stone been thick, it would have been better to have it rise straight from the bottom of the pond. On the other hand, if a stone of this sort is too thin, it should be used only in such places as shoals and sandbars. If there is a considerable difference between the level of the garden and the surface of the water you might build a stone staircase like the one in the photograph to provide a descending passage to the dock.

Figure 94 shows a distant view of the dock in Figure 93. In an ordinary home garden the dock surroundings usually consist of bright lawn or a stone beach so that the water is easily visible from the house. In this case, however, because this is not a dock to be seen from a house the surrounding area is filled with shrubbery.

In Figure 95 there is a dock arranged in a zigzag on pillar stones beyond a stone beach. In relation to the size of the pond and the stone beach, this dock is very small. Although, since the entire stone beach and the dock may be regarded as one, this may be all right, the harmony of the whole would have been more successful if, instead of arranging small narrow stones in a zigzag, one large single stone had been used. In Figure 96, on the other hand, the paved dock on the right is very definitely a dock and harmonizes beautifully with the building. There is variation here because if you view the water from a high place you are struck with its sense of repose, whereas if you come down to the level of the water and look out, vastness is the prevailing impression.

Figure 93.
Dock made of one flat stone.

Figure 94.   Distant view of Figure 93.

Figure 95. Zigzag dock.

Figure 96. Dock paved with cut stones.

Figure 97 (left). Graceful garden island.

Figure 98 (below). Pond with low water level.

F The Island

A garden island must be of such a size that one knows it is a separate island merely by looking at it. A large garden pond might contain an island large enough to walk on, but from the visual viewpoint the island need not be that large. The island in the upper right section of Figure 96 is small but is large enough to look like an island in a garden pond. If you see an island from a distance it looks like an island, but if you go onto it, it no longer does. In a garden, this type of island will not do. Successful examples of islands that do not seem like islands are a special case.

The island in Figure 97 is graceful and charming because all of the base plants are pruned round. Because island vegetation tends to be round, round pruning is suitable on a garden island. In addition, since the pines are low and spread out, this garden island is similar to the real thing. Although the trees on the island on the right are small, it is noteworthy that they do not look like plants in a miniature garden.

In Figure 98, the low water in the pond has left the bottom line of the shore stones exposed. There is no objection to this sort of stone arrangement as a part of a large garden, except that with the bases of the stones exposed we feel something of the atmosphere of a man in a business suit without his pants on. This is not the result of mismanagement of the stones, in this case, but is probably the result of a drought which lowered the pond waters four to six inches. Though it is no great problem to supply a small pond of 10 to 100 square yards with water, a larger pond is more difficult. To prevent a situation like the one in Figure 98, set the stones beforehand with their bases deep as if there were a drought situation, or plant sweet rushes or other water plants around the bases of the stones.

G Pagodas and Stone Lanterns for the Inner Garden

Essentially, pagodas are used in Buddhism to house relics or to serve as memorials, but as you see in Figure 99, there are a number of types and shapes of pagodas that are used as objects of the stone worker's art for the sake of appearance in the inner garden.

There are many cases in which these vertically towering appealing pagodas half hidden, half revealed, play important roles in the garden when they are seen in the distance, placed on top of a mountain or on a mountainside, or in some shrubbery. In these cases, the multi-story tall pagodas are effective.

The so-called treasure tower, which has a compartment for a light, is used near spacious bodies of water, and when the light in it is lit at night its lovliness is difficult to describe. Even in the daytime this type of tower intensifies the atmosphere of being near the water.

Though we don't often see these towers with lights in them, that is what the light compartments are for, and if there are three compartments there should be three lights, and if there are five compartments, five lights. When the towers are lit at night they create a wonderful scene.

There are many types of pagodas including the those with images of the Buddha on four sides of the base, the so-called treasure tower, and those with 28 layers, but since the aesthetic life of them all is their straight-standing verticality, there is not much difference in the way they should all be used.

We shall discuss the setting of these pagodas in a later chapter on garden construction.

Essentially the stone lantern was used in Shinto shrines and in Buddhist temples for votive lights and for roadside illumination, but, like the pagoda, they are used in gardens for their appearance. Their fine shapes and the calm light they give are pleasing, and when their stone surfaces are old and covered with moss, they give an effect of quiet refinement to the entire garden.

With the increase in the demand for these stone lanterns a large number of inferior products have come on the market. It is best to choose a famous old shape. Some of the better types are the Byodo-in, the Bugaku, the Nishinoya, the Yunoki, the Sangatsu-do, the Hannya-ji, the Uzumasa, the Genko-ji, the Renge-ji, the Yahara, the Hokke-ji, the Taima-dera, the Sunsho-an, the Karasumaru, and the Yukimi lanterns. Lanterns of less than 40 inches in height or with no bottom pedestals are usually used in tea gardens, but they may also be used in inner gardens if you do not want the lantern to be conspicuous. Although it is sometimes effective to place a lantern in the middle of a lawn, it is more usual to place them deep in the trees where they can be partially revealed and partially hidden to make the garden seem deeper and more quietly refined.

Since the Yukimi (snow-viewing) lantern has no bottom pedestal but stands on widely spread legs. It should be set on the beach, near the water, or in the water, so that the water or beach is visible through the legs and the lantern gives the effect of a bold straddling stance. Although there are many cases in which the Yukimi lantern is set on top of a flat base stone, this setting conceals the real characteristic feature of the lantern, because if we must set the lantern on a base stone, it would have been better to have used a lantern with a pedestal from the very beginning.

In Figure 101 we see the Yukimi lantern in the garden of the Katsura Detached Palace. In this case the pond provides the background and the shape of the lantern with its large light compartment is informal and pleasant. The thriving moss around the lantern shows that this is a famous old and well-cared-for garden.

Though it is perhaps a little gloomy under the big tree, the absence of base plants around the lantern is good.

In Figure 102 we see a Yaryo lantern in the Katsura Detached Palace garden. Though here again the spreading boughs of the pine are a little gloomy, they are suitable to the symbolism of Shosho-yau, one of the eight famous beautiful scenes in Shosho, China. The lantern itself seems to stand a little dejectedly all alone, but it evokes a feeling of tasteful refinement. The Rakugan lantern in the garden of the Katsura Detached Palace in Figure 103, symbolizes Heisa-raku-gan, another of the eight Chinese scenes mentioned above. The little sandspit that juts resolutely into the pond is interesting, and the beach that is low and close to the level of the water is very refined. Like the old Kinkaku-ji, this garden tastefully represents showy scenery with such small objects as these little lanterns.

The Tamate lantern in Figure 104 stands on a base stone that is too high and that seems vulgar, but placing the lantern at the tip end of the stone is good. Probably this stone was originally placed for the sake of the scene and the lantern was added later.

Much like the sandspit in the pond in the Katsura garden, in the Sunsho-an garden a peninsula-like section of lawn juts out into a raked gravel garden. On the tip end of this lawn section is a Sunsho-an lantern. This is one of the better sections of this garden.

The lantern placed on a flat base in Figure 106 is designed well enough that any place it is set it will look good. There is no objection to setting a lantern on a good flat base because it will then always be accurately placed.

Korean-style pagoda.

Two-story pagoda.

Three-story pagoda.

*Three-story pagoda
with Buddha carvings.*

Figure 99. *Various types of pagoda.*

Five-story treasure tower.

Nine-story pagoda.

Eleven-story pagoda.

Five-story treasure tower.

Nishinoya lantern.

Sangatsu-do lantern.

Byodoin lantern.

Yunoki lantern.

Hannya-ji lantern.

Bugaku lantern.

Uzumasa lantern.

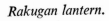

Rakugan lantern.

Yukimi lantern.

Figure 100. Various usual types

Sunsho-an lantern.

Renge-ji lantern.

Hachiman lantern.

Genko-ji lantern.

Yahara lantern.

Koto-ji lantern.

Mina lantern.

Sennyu-ji yukimi lantern.

Omokage lantern.

lanterns for the inner garden.

Figure 101 (left).   Yukimi lantern.

Figure 102 (right).   Yaryo lantern.

Figure 104. Tamate lantern.

Figure 103. Rakugan lantern.

Figure 105. Lantern on a spit of lawn, (Sunsho-an).

Figure 106. Small lantern on a flat base.

H Designs in Raked Gravel

From ancient times, sand has been sprinkled in Japanese gardens. If, as some people think, this did not arise from the miniature tray gardens, at least it is not an importation of a Western attempt to suggest desert landscapes in the garden. From the point of view of gardening techniques, a much more likely explanation lies in the habit of sprinkling Shirakawa gravel or weathered granite gravel in the ancient gardens in Kyoto, where culture budded early. This gravel, which is abundant in the Kyoto district, when spread on the ground gives a clean fresh feeling and does not soil the clothing when one sits on it. The practice of using this gravel to symbolize seascapes is a natural explanation of how the raked patterns came about. Now, of course, the materials are not limited to natural gravel. In addition to a supply of the soft and flaky parts of Shirakawa granite which can be broken into gravel, there are many other types of granite in Japan, such as the reddish variety from the vicinity of the Seto Inland Sea and the yellowish type from Omi Maiko, in Shiga Prefecture. Also, each district has plenty of other types of granite. The selection is not limited to granite, however, any white clean-looking gravel is acceptable. I am fond of using a hardened ash-like stone from Marunuma, in Gumma Prefecture, which is also fine for the purposes of gravel patterns. We can use, then, any type of gravel, white or not, as long as it is fresh and clean looking. There is no reason why Japan, with her long coastline and numerous mountain streams should lack for gravel and sand, and this is true of other countries also. To make the raked pattern clear and precise, however, the gravel must be angular because round pebbles will not stay at the peaks of the ridges of the pattern and do not set the design off well. The virtue of raked gravel is that it vividly brings out the beauty of stone groups, trees, or grasses, and also provides its own neat beauty as a background. White and blue gravel are neat and because they are prominent, they make the area look larger. Black Nachi gravel is imposing, whereas brown Sakuragawa gravel is subdued and refined.

The usual depth of the pattern is between two and four inches. Generally the naked ground is well rolled and the stones are sprinkled on top but when you are using gravel that must be brought from a long way, it is wasteful to lose gravel that sinks into the earth. In such a case lay a base of about three inches of concrete on the ground and then spread the gravel. Although this sort of gravel arrangement will radiate a bit of the midsummer heat, your labor will be cut down because this will be one place where the weeds cannot grow. The usual size of the pebbles is about $\frac{1}{4}$ inch. If the gravel is finer than that, when the weather is in something like a typhoon stage, it will blow about, dance up and down, and ruin the design. If it is too coarse, say $\frac{1}{2}$ inch, it will be difficult to rake the pattern into form.

If asked why rake the gravel into patterns, we might answer:

1. To keep a place that is unsoiled and where no one has walked.
2. To keep moving the gravel so that weeds cannot grow up in it.
3. To keep the garden atmosphere always pure.
4. To keep the gravel even and balanced.
5. To harmonize the gravel patterns with the symbolizing of sand.
6. To give the gravel a type of forcefulness.

Even if the gravel is raked, the footprints of a cat or dog or an inclination for all of the gravel to gather in one thick area makes for a messy feeling. On the other hand, a freshly raked gravel pattern is most refreshing to a guest when he first arrives. A garden that one sees everday can take on a freshness and seem a different place if there is a raked gravel design.

To make a gravel design in a long narrow area, we draw our rake in strokes that parallel and that run with the long narrow plot. Though a steel rake is generally all right to use in this type of work, we usually use a board that is about $\frac{1}{2}$ inch thick, four inches wide, and 16 inches long and that has one flat surface, one surface with sawtooth indentations, and a handle about 60 inches long.

In a spacious area, the basic raking method is to follow the outlines of edging stones, bridges, stone groups, and ditches with a stroke one width of the rake and then to rake the remaining sand in lines that parallel the veranda of the building which the garden faces. If there is a pathway to walk on over the gravel, rake in vertical strokes only around and in the direction of the path. It is also good to describe wave, herring-bone, or arabesque designs in the gravel.

Though the pattern should be uniform and balanced, it is also good to have the pattern conform sometimes to the shape of the terrain. A simple pattern is always better than a complicated one, and directness better than virtuosity, because if the pattern is too involved, it will cease being a pattern and will begin to approach confusion.

It is also essential to choose a pattern that is easy to rake into shape. If the lines of the pattern are parallel to the building, you can draw the rake in one direction going down the plot and then turn and draw it with you as you return.

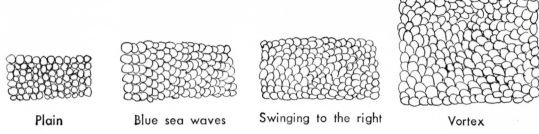

| Plain | Blue sea waves | Swinging to the right | Vortex |

Figure 107. Patterns for spread stones.

This method is economical from a labor viewpoint, and it also prevents the gravel from inclining all in one direction. In the herring-bone pattern push and pull the rake diagonally an arm's length as you go and then repeat the process in the opposite direction as you return. This method, too, is labor saving and prevents the gravel from inclining in one direction. Because the paving stone pattern, on the other hand, requires that each square be done separately, it is inefficient and unsuitable. Patterns of this sort are troublesome and soon come to look neglected and quite ugly because they also provide a good opportunity for the weeds to grow.

ꞌAlthough certainly many people like many different things in gravel patterns so that it has become a custom to find more and more types of patterns, it is necessary to remember that the fundamental psychology of the gravel pattern is neatness and purity and that complicated patterns should not be used as a basis from which to work.

In the words of the gardeners of old, spreading small round stones or coarse gravel of a diameter of from one to two inches is much like sprinkling gravel. This arrangement is not raked, but the stones are lined close with no space between them from one to the next as in the so-called blue-sea-waves fishscale

pattern. In this type of stone arrangement the stones may be spread in the one-directional fishscale pattern, they may be placed so as to form a continuous surface with no pattern, they may all seem to swing in an arc to the right or to the left, or they may be arranged in a vortex (*Figure 107*).

Figure 108 shows an example of a wave pattern in which the gravel seems to move interestingly like light waves.

If the lines seem to move, the sense of quiet will vanish. In Figure 109 we see how, surrounding the stone group with a line is not merely for the sake of outlining the stone group but is also to make the undulations in the pattern look larger. The mixture of straight lines and undulating lines is a little technical and somehow lacks harmonious unity.

In the breakers pattern in Figure 110, the lines in the foreground, which is the side near the house, represent the breakers, while those farther into the garden are the waves out at sea and are raked so that they are horizontally parallel. This is an exemplary instance of using the lively movement of undulating lines for a sense of proximity and the quiet of straight lines for a sense of distance.

Figure 111 shows an instance of a very carefully designed gravel pattern which connects the stones and the moss-covered ground. The over-all scheme is thoroughly planned and matches the stone arrangement very well.

Only the small island-like arrangement of low stones and hair moss is set off by a pattern that follows its outline in the garden in Figure 112. The remaining pattern is in long horizontal lines that parallel the building. This is a well ordered garden arrangement that seems spacious and symbolizes the feeling of exhilaration.

The moon platform in Figure 113 is not merely a gravel pattern, but is a special design which stood next to a similar mound in the Jisho-ji of the Ginkaku-ji. The beauty of this mound is more apparent on a moonlit night or in the twilight than it is in the daytime. These mounds of sand, which have a sort of alluring appeal, are a type of ceremonial devise placed at either side of the entrance to a shrine precinct or at the gate before the carriage stop when a distinguished visitor is expected. They are very reminiscent of the Shinto purification rites in which mounds of salt are put in such places as the gates to the red-light district to ward off impurity. From this hint, these mounds were exaggerated and put in gardens to foster purity of the soul and to provide a shining quiet view in the blue of an early moonlit night. Because the Japanese people, who are found of cleanliness and purity, have continued to use this type of pure element, not found any-where else, in their gardens from ancient times to the present, the moon platform must be called an outstanding piece of Japanese garden design.

In Figure 114 we see several round moss patches in an area of raked gravel which gives a particularly well planned effect. The floating quiet beauty of the moss is enhanced by leaving the gravel in no particular pattern. The contrast between the moss and the gravel is particularly skilfully managed.

The stone arrangement and gravel and lawn garden in Figure 115 is at the training ground for the Chuo Railroad. Although using the Shirakawa gravel with its prominent coloration in the rear, makes the background look too near, because a white gravel garden is much too glaring under the hot Kanto Plains sun, the grass section is in the front to act as a kind of filter. The *hiba* in the back are pruned in a straight line and are refreshing with the stone arrangement. When they grow taller and thicker they will make a fine background. Planted close up against the *hiba*, there is a row of *matsurika* which should be kept pruned to set the stone arrangement off to good effect. Instead of making the boundary between the lawn and the stone garden a straight line, it was curved to hug the building because a curved line seems more intimate when viewed from the building. If the line had been straight it would have overpowered the building and would have been unpleasant.

Though raking the gravel to follow the lines of the greenery and the stones in their vicinity and raking the remaining sand parallel with the lines of the building's garden would have been appropriate in this case, actually no raked pattern at all has been used.

The combination of pruned shrubbery and raked sand in Figures 116 and 117 is interesting and pleasant because nothing but simple parallel lines has been used and there is not a trace of technical trickery. The gravel and the shrubbery symbolize a cheerful mood and are harmoniously effective. With these simple base plants the quieter refined Sakuragawa gravel is more suitable than Shirakawa gravel, but since Sakuragawa gravel is round and has few edges and angles it does not stand as clearly in a pattern as Shirakawa gravel does.

The seedling stones and gravel garden in Figure 118 is in front of the bathroom in the Marunuma Spa Hotel in Gumma Prefecture. In this district there are a number of varieties of mountain stones, with seedling plants growing in their crevices, which in this arrangement have been treated as islands and stones in the water and have been surrounded by white weathered ash-like gravel of about $\frac{1}{8}$ inch, which has been spread in uniform layers. When this gravel is wet it turns yellowish white, and when it is dry it is a bluish white. Because the stone is naturally uniform and since the location is near the source there are no impurities in it, and layers of over 40 inches are easy to find.

The garden was set deep and the stones and gravel elevated somewhat so that they could be easily seen by people sitting in the bath. In the raked gravel there are islands of mosses, and the plants are primarily Japanese yew and low pines. The base plants are various mountain grasses. There is *shakunage* behind the large stone in the inner section. The large stump on the left was brought from the swamps where it was an obstacle in a road. The freshness of the raked gravel garden against such an object from the primeval forests makes a nice view for those who are entering the bath.

Figure 119 shows a combination of a stream bordered with larger stones (about three inches) with a narrow band of Shirakawa gravel only in the stream itself. Later we reconsidered and thought it would have been better to use the larger stones set low in place of the Shirakawa gravel which has become discolored with slime. Because if there is very little water in the stream it will only cover the bottoms of the stones and will not be visible from the surface, you might spread a low layer of mortar and let the water flow over that.

Figure 108.   Raked gravel in a wave pattern.

(*opposite page*)
Figure 109 (*above*).
Gravel raked in waving and straight lines.

Figure 110 (*below*).
Gravel in a breaker pattern.

Figure 111.   Well planned gravel, stone, and moss design.

Figure 112. Moss island set in raked gravel.

Figure 113.   Moon platform.

Figure 114. Round patches of moss in raked gravel.

Figure 115. Lawn with gravel and stone garden.

Figure 116.   Raked gravel and pruned shrubbery.

Figure 117.   Raked gravel and a pine surrounded with pruned shrubbery.

Figure 118.
Seedling stones and gravel garden seen from a hot springs bath.

Figure 119. Stream spread with gravel and bordered with larger stones.

PART TWO

Special Gardens

The Courtyard Garden

§1 *The Function and Essentials of the Courtyard Garden*

BECAUSE the function of the courtyard garden is to improve the lighting and ventilation of the room that faces onto it, it is essential to avoid planting in it large luxuriant trees that would darken the room. It is better to plant trees with scant foliage such as the bamboo, the windmill palm, Japanese banana, the dracaena, and the coconut palm. If the courtyard garden is insufficiently lit, it might be completely converted into a pond garden with stepping stones, into a stone and sand garden, or into a simple garden consisting of a single stone and a single tree.

Though the usual garden is out of doors, there are many instances in which the courtyard garden is not. Sometimes the courtyard differs from a real room only in that it is lacking a roof and for this reason can be quite different from other types of gardens. Although, naturally, you cannot use the courtyard garden as an ordinary room when it is raining or when it is hot enough for air-conditioning or cold enough for heating, but in ordinary good weather, it can serve for eating, reading, or entertaining. Treating the courtyard garden as a roofless room, you might pave a section of it with tiles, roofing tiles, or paving stones and set tables and chairs in it as you would in an ordinary room. Since one of the main charms of this type of garden lies in the idea of a roofless room where one may enjoy Nature under the magnificent sky, we must take care not to plant unreasonably large plants where there is insufficient sunlight or to set large stones where there is only a little space, because doing this destroys the possibility of using the garden as a room. There are, of course, exceptional cases. For instance, if there is no other garden and you want to have something like a garden or if you have plenty of interior room in your house and you do not really need a roofless room, then it is perfectly all right to use gravel and stones or to plant trees that can take shade well.

Figure 120.   Courtyard garden at the Burmese Embassy in Tokyo.

Moreover, if your neighborhood is such that your house can be seen into from the roofs of neighboring houses and you would like to be able to enjoy a little more privacy, plant thick trees in your courtyard garden to obstruct the view, then you can put a hammock there and doze or go around in little clothing to cool off when the weather is hot.

§2   An Example of a Courtyard Garden

In the photograph of the courtyard garden at the Burmese Embassy (*Figure 120*) we see one section that is planted while the remaining sections are left empty of trees with luxuriant foliage. Since this garden is large for a courtyard garden, it would have been better to plan it farther inward, but this arrangement was chosen out of respect for the architectural view.

CHAPTER TWO

The Interior Garden

§ 1　*The Function and Essentials of the Interior Garden*

THE INTERIOR garden is an artificial garden made to ornament such confined spaces as the area beneath a staircase. It has no practical function but is intended to introduce something of natural scenery into the structure of the interior and to create a sense of freshness. Even though it is not feasible to keep trees fresh inside the house, an interior garden can feature stones or sand in their natural conditions. In any event, since this is a type of garden for confined spaces, it is safest to use only a few stones and an art object for accent.

When you want a garden but lack the spare outdoor space for one, you might arrange a stone group of thin stones along an interior wall to suggest a waterless stream or you might even replace a wall with a waterless-stream-type natural stone arrangement and then fill in the crevices with some type of wall material for an interesting design. It is safer, however, to make a neat and simple stone arrangement that is not too heavy looking. You might also introduce a natural atmosphere into your interior by using natural stones or logs with the bark on them for columns, by making an interior staircase out of natural stones, by putting stepping stones in a corridor, or by using a garden water basin or a stone lantern inside the house.

A characteristic feature of the art of gardening lies in the presence as a part of the garden, no matter how small it is, of the boundless sky above. The interior garden, however, is isolated and cut off from the sky and has no connection with the wind, snow, rain, or clouds. It does not become a part of the combined natural elements, the sun, moon, stars, and the weather. Moreover, stones outside become covered with frost and with moss which hide their crudeness, but the stones in an interior garden display their crudeness openly and tend to look affected. For this reason, it is safer to avoid stones that are too rough or too ornamental.

Figure 121.   Interior garden at the Burmese Embassy, Tokyo.

§2   *An Example of an Interior Garden*

Figure 121 shows the interior garden at the Burmese Embassy with a small pond containing stones. The water from this small pond falls down one step and flows into the courtyard garden pond. It would also be easy to achieve success-ful results with some such other simple method as placing a stone, a piece of sculpture, or some other stone or ceramic art object on an area spread with sand.

CHAPTER THREE

The Rooftop Garden

§1 *The Function and Essentials of the Rooftop Garden*

THE ROOFTOP garden attempts to convert the rooftop, which is removed from the ground, back into a segment of the ground and to bring some of the joy of nature into an hygienic environment. This means, in essence, that its use is roughly the same as that of the interior garden. Since this garden is on the top of a building and is exposed to the wind, it is impossible to use tall weak trees or heavy cumbersome stones. It is more profitable to design these gardens around small plants, artistic undulations of surface, light stone arrangements, and gravel raked into patterns.

As we have said before, the rooftop garden, because of its placement on a building top, does not permit the free use of large trees and mammoth stones the way the ordinary inner garden does. In place of this, it is important to enliven the view, which in this case is a main feature of the garden. The noisy dirty streets of the city, become a type of scenery when one is removed about 100 or 200 yards from them. We must say that it is the magic of the atmosphere, but when one looks down through a few hundred yards of the open air, the rooftops, the telephone poles, and the electric wires of the streets below become a scene to watch and the trolleys and trains running along the streets are an accessory of motion to a rooftop garden.

In a rooftop garden, because it is important to use all of the limitless sky in the content of the garden, you should plant a green lawn and use low shrubbery that will not obstruct the view of the sky. Using white sand, near-white stones, or white covering stones, hurts the eyes in the bright sunlight and is a design that does not take advantage of the open air. The roots of plants are frail and over a long period of time they will exude acid which will in turn corrode concrete or other building materials. To prevent this, put a layer of plate glass or some other anticorrosive material under the garden soil.

§2 An Example of a Rooftop Garden

The photograph of a pond skilfully harmonized with right angles (*Figure 122*) is of a section of the rooftop garden on the top of the Yasuda Insurance Building, across the street from the west entrance to Shinjuku station in Tokyo. The whole is unified by making the straight lines of the pond and all the other straight lines parallel those of the building. A lightweight arrangement of stones from Mt. Amagi and the pruned *hiba* hedge behind it block part of the sky in Figure 123. This type of stone is not a strain on the building's structure, and if the bottom should jut out and make setting difficult, you can easily cut off the unwanted parts. Although, in this case, azaleas were planted around the bases of the stone and left untrimmed, it would also have been interesting if they had been pruned round. A single winter camellia used in its natural shape as an accessory is also good. The stone arrangement seems to come to life in contrast with the straight lines of the pruned plants.

The pruned flower garden and the white sand garden in Figure 124 were mentioned earlier. The white sand and stone arrangement seen roughly in the center is called "*demon and children*": and is explained in the chapter on stone arranging. The appealing shape of the urn in the pruned flower garden is quite effective.

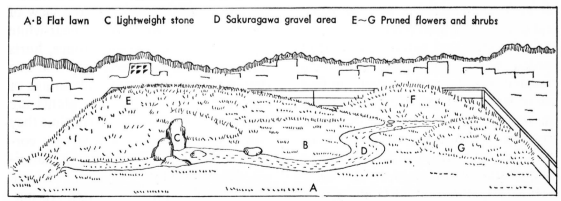

A·B Flat lawn   C Lightweight stone   D Sakuragawa gravel area   E~G Pruned flowers and shrubs

Over-all plan of a rooftop garden.

Figure 122. Pond designed to harmonize with right angles.

Figure 123. Pruned plants against the sky.

Figure 124.   Garden with pruned flowerbeds, gravel, and stones.

CHAPTER FOUR

The Garden Below the Floor

§1 *Function and Essentials of Gardens below the Floor*

IN THIS section, when we speak of gardens below the floor, we do not mean the continuation of another type of garden into the area under a floor. We mean a garden that can be seen from a half-basement room in a building that has a fairly high floor level. Since by definition, this space below the floor is drearily unpleasant, the purpose of putting a garden there is to change this gloomy area into a pleasant scene and to provide psychological food for thought. Because this is an area that is difficult to keep clean, cleanliness in the garden is essential. Moreover, plants will not grow under the floor, and since modern artificial flowers, even though they so closely resemble the real thing, are not adequate for a sense of the real joy of a garden, something in the line of a natural stone and sand arrangement is necessary. Even in the places in which you might place a stone lantern or a piece of sculpture, we need to see something natural like a little gravel spread around.

Although, in the sense that the garden for the area under the floor is an interruption in an interior space, it resembles the interior garden, from the lighting viewpoint, the conditions of this garden are one step worse. On the other hand, I believe that anyone who is fond of gardens has experienced to some extent the feeling that a garden seen at twilight is more refined than one with a large number of gaudy stone arrangements seen in the bright daylight. Because the garden under the floor is seen always in a light similar to that of dusk, in this sense, its conditions are pleasing. With this type of pale dark lighting atmosphere, we can create a refined garden even using gaudy materials. Brightly colored beautiful red and blue stones arrangements in an ordinary out-of-doors garden tend to be too flashy and to look unsettled. Using these bright stones in a garden under the floor will decidedly look settled, refined, and somewhat mysterious because of the poor lighting.

Figure 125.   Garden below the floor at Mr. N's home.

§2   *An Example of a Garden below the Floor*

This is the under-floor garden in the home of Mr. N, as it is seen from the half-basement entranceway. White Shirakawa gravel was spread out to give a somewhat brighter feeling to this dark area. A low stone lantern in the middle of the white sand, a lantern hollowed from a single piece of stone, or an appealing piece of sculpture in the newer style would also have suited this type of under-floor garden.

CHAPTER FIVE

The Alleyway Garden

§1 *The Function and Essentials of the Alleyway Garden*

THE ALLEYWAY garden, which is to be looked at as we walk along, is used in narrow passages, where the view is directed downward, rather than in open spaces. This type of garden must create a pleasant scene without obstructing the way, since convenience is the function of these narrow passages. Because, while walking along, we could only see the base and column of a large lantern, a small stone lantern, visible in its entirety, is preferable. Sometimes, perhaps we might like to create a sort of tunnel of greenery in these narrow spaces, but usually there is not enough margin of land to plant large trees, and a connecting walkway made of stepping stones, rectangular stones, or stones with crests carved on their upper surfaces is more desirable. If plants are planted, they should be something like the bamboo with small roots, for instance *shiho* bamboo, arrow bamboo, *narihira* bamboo, daimyo bamboo, *taimin* bamboo, *kan* bamboo, or perhaps nandina, Dutch rush, *tachibana*, spear flower, or ferns, which are plants that add elegance to the alleyway gardens.

§2 *An Example of an Alleyway Garden*

This is an extremely plain alleyway garden made of nothing but round paving stones arranged in a straight line, with some swept gravel to the side. If you would like something more scenic than this simple garden, you might use stones, or perfectly flat stepping stones with rectangular stones or stones with carved crests in between them for variety. On the left in Figure 126 and running along the fence, you might plant some *shiho* bamboo or *kan* bamboo. A small stone footpath lantern in the upper left in the picture might also be good.

Figure 126. An alleyway garden with paving stones.

CHAPTER SIX

The Tea Garden

§1 *The Function and Essentials of the Tea Garden*

THE TEA garden, or the *roji* as it is also called, serves to improve the environment for the performance of the tea ceremony. To this end, it must contain a water basin in which to ritually wash away the uncleanliness and the cares of the world from the spirit, a quiet and composed stone lantern for illumination when guests wash their hands at night, and it must be divided from the other garden areas by the simplest of fences.

The classical tea gardens of old were divided into three stages: the outer *roji*, the middle *roji*, and the inner *roji*.

In the outer *roji*, on the way to the inner *roji*, there is an ornamental toilet and a real toilet. The middle *roji* serves as a place to rest in during the interval after the guests have entered the tea house in the inner *roji* once and have partaken of the tea and light refreshments there. In this garden there should be a sort of neutral waiting area and, if there are no ornamental and real toilets in the outer *roji*, they will be found in the middle *roji*.

The inner *roji* is the ultimate in garden *shibusa* and reflects the attitude of harmonious human relations and simple refinement about which we spoke in the introduction. When one enters this garden, he leaves the cares and trouble of the vulgar world behind and steps into the land of serene light—another name, in fact, for this inner garden. That is to say, this garden must represent what is the ideal land to the Buddhist and what is Heaven to the Christian. To highlight the refinement of the inner garden, the middle garden should be elegant, and the outer garden either slightly mysterious or an ordinary sunny garden.

Regardless of where a gardener plans the walkways in a public garden, the people are sure to walk in another nearby area and make the real pathway obsolete. This is, in a way, the public's criticism of the garden itself. Of course it is necessary to attempt proper walkway planning, but when it comes to the tea garden for a true tea ceremony,

(Today an abbreviated version is used.) the majority of the things one has so assiduously learned have a tendency to become abbreviated. This, in a sense, could be viewed as public criticism of the tea ceremony for not surpassing real life in compactness. From this viewpoint, in constructing the tea garden it would be an improvement to use the middle garden as an approach to the entrance for distinguished guests and to do away with the *nijiriguchi*, the small, low door through which guests must enter the teahouse. Nevertheless, it is better that only the most distinguished guests may enter the distinguished guests' entrance as comfortably as those heavenly beings who existed in the age before man was created, and that the remaining humbler guests must enter the low, narrow *nijiriguchi*. Were there to be no *nijiriguchi*, the significance of the distinguished guests' entrance would vanish, and nothing would remain but a mere entranceway. This conforms to our daily lives in which it is the main aim of coarser men and women to purify themselves of the despicable through humility.

On the other hand, even if this distinction between the noble and the humble guests should disappear, the main aim of the tea ceremony, self purification, and the esteem for the refinement of the ceremony would not change, because in these things lie the significance and the reason for the endurance of the tea ceremony itself.

Because the beauty of the refinement of the tea ceremony avoids the symbolization of worldly desires, such glittering things as gold are opposed to its tastes. Anything is suitable for the ceremony as long as it is plain and humble. It is not necessary to use only cheap things, but just as the water in the ritual basin is scant, so should the dignified elements in the garden be few. Even though the light meal before the tea ceremony is not of the finest delicacies of land and sea, it is essential that it be warm to the degree that warming stones can make it, so that it will surpass all time.

The taste of the tea master enables him to choose objects of dignity and refinement from among a group of coarse things, but the general person, whose eye, when confronted with a rich display of high-quality articles, is likely to be lead by the price, will find it difficult to select a fine piece from a group of cheap items. To give real examples, however, if one is choosing garden basins or lanterns that are quite old and have a history, they may cost as much as from two to three thousand dollars, but good copies of the famous old pieces made by men who understand the stone cutter's art may be bought for less than three hundred dollars. Of course this is more expensive than the ordinary type of lantern or basin that sell for around one hundred dollars, but this is an inevitable situation. Since a dim light, like the Buddhist serene light, is more suitable to the dark *shibusa* of the *roji*, it is essential to plan the garden in a place that is partially hidden from the sun. If you water the plants and stones in such a half shaded garden faithfully morning and evening, the entire garden will become covered in a moss that is particulary suited to the mood of refinement of a tea garden.

In recent times, for the sake of people from other countries who do not find it comfortable to sit on the tatami in the Japanese fashion, a standing chair tea ceremony has developed for the preparing and drinking of the tea, but if this is not done in a tea garden one cannot fully enjoy the pleasure of the ceremony. Even if the garden is not divided into three stages or if there is not even an inner garden, if there is a basin and a lantern in the room, even only a summer portable lantern, one can perform the tea ceremony. Nevertheless, it is much better to make the garden and the alcove as refined as possible.

The wash basin and the tea garden wash basin, or *tsukubai*, play the leading role in the tea garden, and we shall discuss them in a later chapter.

§2 *Suitable Trees for the Inner* Roji

Such gorgeous flowering plants as the bull bay, the camellia, the pomegranate, and the cherry, because they do not suit the refined feeling of the garden and because they cannot be well arranged in the tea house, are not suitable for the inner *roji*. All of the wind-pollinated flowers, however, have an elegant simplicity and are quite all right in this garden. Some of the insect-pollinated plants, too, like the *hisakagi*, the Japanese pittosporum, the Arabian jasmin, the *hiiragi*, and the raphiolepis among the evergreens, or the Japanese beauty berry, the *shiroshikibu*, the *gamazumi*, the fine-tooth holly, the *dodan*, the winged spindle tree, the elder, the winter jasmine, and the Japanese witch-hazel, among the deciduous plants, or any plant with flowers that are small, white, lavender or any inconspicuous color will fit in the inner *roji*.

For a ground covering and around the stepping stones and the water basin, you should use the hairmoss, the pondweed, and the *muku-muku-chirimen* moss the gardeners popularly call ground mosses. Shirakawa gravel is fine in the outer and middle *roji*, but it does not suit the inner *roji*. Although there are instances in which we can use Sakuragawa gravel in the inner *roji*, it does not always fit the refined mood and is better used in the middle *roji*.

Stones for the inner *roji* should be of the types that will take moss and evoke a feeling of refinement easily. Granite, andesite, diorite and tufa, are good. Gaudy red, blue, or white stones such as those with high iron deposites, chrolite schist, or ashy stones, are far from being composed enough to suit the refinement of the inner *roji*, and one should definitely avoid them.

§3 *Stone Lanterns Suitable to the Inner* Roji

We shall speak later of the tea garden water basin, but since the stone lantern is in the garden to illuminate this basin, we shall discuss it now. It is best to choose a lantern that is under 60 inches in height and that has a certain amount of dignity and is not overly carved or ornamented. Other than that, the choice of the lantern is up to the tastes of the owner of the garden. Some lanterns without pedestals that suit the refined feeling of the tea garden are the Oribe lantern, the Mizuhotaru lantern, the Rikyu-konomi lantern, the Domyo-ji lantern, the Koetsu lantern, the Shuko lantern, and the Shueki lantern. Some other lanterns that can be used if their pedestals are buried are the Yunoki lantern, the Nishiya lantern, the Taima-dera lantern, the Rikuso-an lantern, and the Renge-ji lantern. Such a lantern as the Daibutsu lantern has a sufficiently refined shape and is low enough that it can be used just as it is. There are enough refined lanterns available that it is always better to avoid the ones that have complicated carving.

Around the bending path stones at the entrance of the garden it is best to use some low lantern like the Tamate lantern, the Sunsho-an lantern, or the Tengajaya lantern to light the foot path.

Heavily carved lanterns are used as mountain lanterns, but there are few among them that have any real dignity. A single stone with a light compartment cut out of it would serve better and give a nicer feeling to the garden.

Guide stone

Oribe lantern

Taima lantern

Rikyu lantern

Shokin lantern

Domyo-ji lantern

Koshin lantern

Figure 127. Lanterns suitable for the roji.

Oribe-konomi lantern

Roji lantern

Mizuhotaru lantern

Guide stone

Kakuashimoto lantern

Rikyu lantern

Koetsu lantern

Boulder-shape lantern.

Tamate lantern.

Chinese-type lantern.

Tengajaya lantern.

Sunsho-an lantern.

Figure 128.   Suitable inner roji lanterns.

§4 *Suitable* Roji *Path Stones*

For stepping stones in the *roji*, stones that are not too hard, of the andesite group, coffer stones, or Ise granite are good. For paving, granite stones with earth in the cracks between them and covered with moss are suitable. Flag stones, particularly those from the Tamba district, have a nice color and grain, but since they are thin they must be joined with mortar. In addition, if they are pure black they are overly pretty and do not suit a *roji*. If you must use these flag and pure black stones, create a disorderly line of greenery and pave with the stones so that they will have a certain degree of refinement. Though the color of the hexagonal stones from Kamishima, one of the Izu Islands near Tokyo, is refined, they seem very hard and are out of place in the *roji*. The same thing can be said about a variety of other types of stones often inset under buildings.

To make the sense of quiet refinement in the inner *roji* more keenly perceptible, make the middle *roji* a fairly pretty garden. Since the main aim of the two is to make the middle *roji* elegant and the inner *roji* tastefully refined, a bamboo or a sand garden is suitable for the middle *roji*. A lot of luxuriant trees or colorful flowers would definitely be out of place. Since the garden should have life, subdued plants and stones are advisable. Because just flag stones or plain black stones are obviously purely paving, brighten them up with an occasional rectangular stone or a stepping stone with a crest on it.

In the outer *roji*, which is a purely ordinary garden, beautiful flowers and trees, lawns, ponds, or streams are all quite fine. Of course, in the case of a stream it is completely acceptable to run the stream from the outer *roji* into the middle *roji* and from there into the inner *roji*, but as the stream passes through these gardens it must become elegant to suit the middle *roji*, and quietly refined to suit the inner *roji*.

§5   *The* Tsukubai *Basin Front*

Because the primary role of the inner *roji* is to provide a place in which to ritually wash the cares and dirt of the world from one's soul, there is a ritual water basin in the garden. This water basin is called a *tsukubai* from the Japanese word *tsukubau* which means to crouch, because one must bend over to use the water in the *tsukubai*. To make removing the used water from the basin easier, the ground in front of the *tsukubai* is one level lower than the garden level. This depression is called the "sea" of the *tsukubai* and is surrounded with stones. The entire area around the *tsukubai* is called the *tsukubai* basin front.

In the chart in Figure 129 we see the *tsukubai* basin front with the names of the stones, their placement and heights, the depth of the "sea," and other pertinent information. If we take the height of the garden to be ± 0, the stepping stones should be more than $1\frac{1}{2}$ inches high, and the front stone should be set at about the same or, perhaps, one inch higher. This is an ordinary setting. There are also instances in which the stones are arranged to descend, with the front stone set lower than the stepping stone so that one must step down to it. The *yuoke* (hot-water bucket) stone on the right is normally set two inches higher

than the front stone, but it may also be set lower. This stone is set this way so that it will be in easy reach of the right hand of a person squatting on the front stone. The *teshoku* (hand illuminating) stone on the left is set four inches higher than the front stone to be in easy reach of the left hand of a person squatting on the front stone. This stone is thought to be set high to put the hand in better light. Although the *yuoke* stone could be placed lower than the front stone, that is, on a level with the surface of the ground, from a balance viewpoint this would make an awkward arrangement in which the *yuoke* and the *teshoku* stones would be of the same heights. It is better to maintain at least some height variation between these stones. Even though, if you have an interesting *teshoku* stone and would like to set it as high as possible, it must not be so high that it overpowers the water basin, which after all, is the principal feature of the group. The prop stone behind the water basin is set so as to seem to look out over the basin when it is set in the middle of the "sea"; however, if the basin is set to the back so that there is a "sea" only in the front, there is no need for this stone. Even when the basin is in the middle, the back of it should be between four and eight

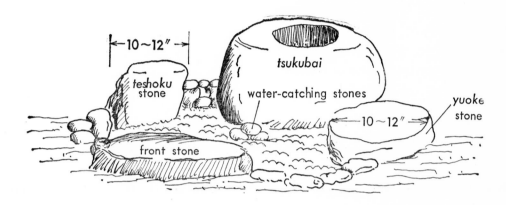

Figure 129.   Over-all sketch of tsukubai *water basin front.*

inches from the rear wall of the "sea." The customary distance from the front stone to the water in the basin is about 24 inches.

Although the depth of the "sea" varies in accordance with the height of the water basin—if the basin is taller, the "sea" is deeper—the standard is about 80 to 120 inches. If the basin is a carved one, it should stand on a pedestal stone. If, on the other hand, it is merely a stone with a hole cut out of it, it may be set directly into the "sea" with into the "sea" with no pedestal.

The basin should not be more than eight inches taller than the front stone, because if it is, when in use its water will seem smaller and it will be difficult to use. Make the "sea" deep and set the basin deep into it so that the difference between the front stone and the basin heights is between eight and ten inches. There are several large stones piled in front of the basin to hide the water drainage hole underneath. In the place of stones you might also use some old tiles.

§6   *Water for the* Tsukubai

There are two methods of getting water into the *tsukubai*. The tea ceremony host's assistant, or the *hanto*, may bring the water to the *tsukubai* on the day of the ceremony on three seperate occasions: just before the guests arrive, before the interval, and just before the conclusion of the ceremony. However,

there is a device, the *kakehi*, which constantly pours water into the water basin. Finally we complete the *tsukubai* arrangement by spreading the "sea" with gravel of a uniform diameter of eight to twelve inches or we might pave it with small stones.

In Figure 130 there is a basin front in which the *yuoke* stone has been reduced in size because the stone on which the pillar on the right rests balances the *teshoku* stone. The real *yuoke* stone is much smaller and to the side. Putting the *yuoke* stone, on top of which a bucket (*oke*) of hot water (*yu*) for winter use is put, directly on top of the paving stones is interesting. A *kakehi* is used with this basin.

Figure 131 shows a basin front in which former building foundation stones have been used. Using a round foundation stone for a front stone is an interesting touch. The *yuoke* stone and the *teshoku* stone are set in the usual fashion, and there are stones to hide the drain in front of the basin. Because the hole in this basin is very large, it must be quite a task for the host's assistant to pour in the water. It is usual when the mouth of a basin is either excessively large or excessively small to use a *kakehi*. If the hole is too large, there is a great deal of work involved in filling the basin. If it is too small, the water in the basin will be sufficient for only about five guests. Though the aspidistra and Japanese aralia planted in front of the front stone and the round stones set there may seem a little tasteless, the over-all result

is good.

In Figure 132 of an iron-pot shaped *tsukubai*, the large bent stone in the rear right is a little irritating, but the luxuriant ferns around it save it. It is good that the stone in the rear of the *tsukubai* is large, low, and quiet, because it could be conspicuous enough to overpower the *tsukubai* from a user's viewpoint. It is essential to maintain the hero and supporting-actor relationship between this stone and the water basin. In addition, don't turn the ladle face-down as in the picture. Turn it so that its mouth faces left. This is a different type of placement from that used in the teahouse itself.

The poles sunk at random at the sides of the mortar *tsukubai* in Figure 133 are highlighted with Dutch rush which suits them very well. The *Koetsu* lantern is appropriate to a well-crib *tsukubai*, though a hexagonal one would not be.

The boulder-shape basin in Figure 134 is interesting against the bamboo fence, but the stone on the left is too close and seems a little tumultuous. In Figure 135, a test for proper heights of the stones, we see that both the *teshoku* stone and the *yuoke* stone are too high and overpower the basin, which should be the main feature of the arrangement, so that the whole thing is out of balance. This could be remedied and a certain composure achieved, if the *teshoku* stone were lowered to a point half way between the heights of the basin and the front stone and if the *yuoke* stone were lowered to a point halfway between the heights of the *teshoku* stone and the front stone.

In addition to the setting in the center or to the rear of the "sea," there are any number of other ways to set the *tsukubai*. For instance, you might set it in a stream or in a pond, you might set the front stone a level lower than the garden and make a two- or three-step staircase down to the front stone, you might catch the water from a fountain with a small *kakehi* and let the water accumulate in between the rocks. You might also have a basin into which fresh spring water drips little by little, or you might put the basin in a spring so that to reach the basin you must cross a series of stepping stones. According to your own tastes, there is a wide selection of variations you could work on the *tsukubai* arrangement.

If, when the tea ceremony host's assistant, whom we mentioned earlier, brings the buckets of water to refill the basin before the guests arrive and during the interval, he will let the basin overflow a while, it will be unnecessary to remove the old water for the basin water to become clean. When we put the water into the basin just before the interval in the tea ceremony we make a sound with the water loud enough to be faintly audible to the guests inside the teahouse. The sound of the water is a signal to the guests to prepare themselves spiritually for the interval.

Tsukubai come in any number of shapes. There is the natural rock shape which has a natural hole in the top, there is the natural rock into which a hole has been cut for the water, there are the four-sided and the six-sided *tsukubai* with images of the Buddha carved on the sides, there are the *tsukubai* made from the central sections of the *Gorin*-type stone tower or the *Taho*-type stone tower, there is the *tsukubai* called the *kesagata*, or priest's-mantle shape, because it bears a carved design resembling that on a priest's mantle, there is the Ginkaku-ji style with geometric carvings, the Taima-dera basin, the Fusen basin, and the temple-stone basin. Among these basins, the ones that are from 20 to 28 inches in height are most suitable for a tea garden. Although we can use larger basins and make the "sea" deeper, the taller basins are more suited to a *shoin*-style tea garden or to an ordinary veranda.

The hole in the basin is usually cut so that the diameter halfway down is from 1.1 to 1.3 times as large as the diameter of the mouth so that when the hole is filled with water the light rays will be refracted and make the hole look deeper. Although a hemispheric hole is also good, because when it is filled it looks like a shallow dish, the deeper method with the mouth diameter smaller than the mid-diameter is more natural and refined. Sometimes the bottom of the hole in the basin is flat, like a well crib, but the water does not look at all good in this type of hole. There are many shapes for the hole in the basin, including the round, the pile, the square, the diamond, and the gourd shapes, but it is better to make at least the bottom of the hole round because this makes changing the water easier.

Sometimes five to $\frac{1}{2}$ inch lower than the rim of the hole there is a 1- or $1\frac{1}{2}$-inch ledge which, showing through the shallow water a level lower than the edge of the hole, is pleasant to see. If you want this type of ledge, do not make it as narrow as $\frac{1}{2}$-$\frac{3}{4}$ inch because this will look too fussy for a basin that should be simple. Unlike the cases of fountains or bird baths, because if there is no moss around the *tsukubai*, its feeling of tasteful refinement will not materialize, it is usual to place these basins among deep shady trees. The plants around the basin should be the types that insects do not particularly like, that are harmless, and that do not make an unpleasant odor. Some very suitable plants for this purpose are the *asebo*, the ring-cupped oak the Arabian jasmine, the rapliolepis, the

tachibana, the spear flower, and the *kakuremino*. The *hisakagi* attracts a caterpillar that turns into a poisonous moth, but since this plants are so refined and tasteful, they are often used. The caterpillars can be easily taken care of with a chemical insecticide. Because too many of the same evergreens becomes tedious you might also use some of the deciduous plants like the *dodan* or the *natsuhaze*, both of which are quite in good taste.

Usually winter camellias and trees and shrubs that flower with overly beautiful flowers are not used around the *tsukubai*. If on the other hand, the *tsukubai* is large and has a spring running constantly from it, or if the basin-front arrangement is in front of a magnificent drawing room, you may use any type of gorgeous flower you wish and treat the *tsukubai* much the way you would treat a fountain. For instance in such a case you might use peonies, Chinese peonies, winter camellias, or the larger chrysanthemums. Still it is always safer to use small white or lavendar flowers around the *tsukubai*, because it is essentially associated with the tea ceremony and the tea house where it is quite all right for the flowers to be of less importance. In this sense, even if the plants are of the wind-polinated varieties, their flowers should be simple.

The dipper used at the *tsukubai* is usually made of a layer of thin wood bent

Figure 130. Tsukubai *basin front with a reduced* yuoke *stone.*

into a round cup with a diameter of 3 inches and a depth of 2½ inches. The handle should be measure about ½ inch at the base, ⅓ inch by ½ inch at the outer end, and be 16 inches long. As we have said before, this dipper should be placed on the *tsukubai* with the mouth to the left. This is done to provide variation from the way of placing the dipper on the container in the tearoom, where it is either turned mouth down or mouth up. It is polite, however, to put the dipper back the way the host himself placed it, if he has chosen some other method of placement. It is permissible to place the dipper directly on the basin, but it is better to make a rack for it from two joined pieces of bamboo cut longer than the basin is wide and bound with bracken or vines. Put this rack on the inner side of the basin and put the dipper on top of it. If you use bamboo, use green bamboo for a fresh feeling.

Figure 131 (left).
Basin made from an old foundation stone.

Figure 132 (top right).
Basin shaped like a steel pot.

Figure 133 (second from top).
Basin made from a mortar stone.

Figure 134 (third from top).
Basin in water-pot shape.

Figure 135 (bottom right).
Checking the heights of the various stones.

Iron-pot-shaped basin.

Basin with the six images of Buddha.

Basin with the four images of Buddha.

Saltpan basin.

Fusen basin.

Figure 136. Various tsukubai *basins.*

Boulder-shaped basin.

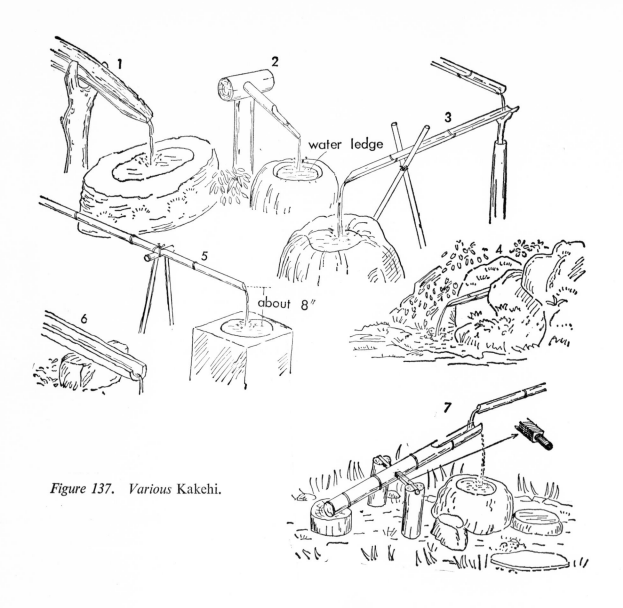

Figure 137. Various Kakehi.

§8 *The* Kakehi

In Figures 138 and 139 we see the *sozu kakehi*, an interesting type of *kakehi*. The water flows down one length of bamboo into another which is closed at the bottom end to form a bottle-like object and which is suspended on pins so that it can swing freely. Then the water from the first bamboo pipe fills the bottom one, the bottom one tips end up and empties the water into the pond, basin, or stream, making a clacking sound as it falls. Figure 138 shows a *sozu kakehi* set in a small pond, not near a *tsukubai*. Figure 139 shows another of them from the top. There is a sketch of this *kakehi* in number seven in Figure 137. Number one in Figure 137 is a *kakehi* made of natural wood, number two is an ordinary *kakehi*, number three is a double layered *kakehi*, number four is a *kakehi* that constantly supplies fresh water in quantity, number five is a round bamboo *kakehi*, and number six is a stone *kakehi*.

Figure 138. A sozu kakehi.

Figure 139. A sozu kakehi *seen from above.*

§9 *The* Chiriana *and the Inset Stone*

In Figure 140 we see the *chiriana*, or trash hole, which is intended to be a place where guests at the tea ceremony ritually throw away the unclean things from their spirits. It is not a place to throw real trash but is a kind of ornamental hole into which green pine needles or black tea branches are put on occasions when there is a tea ceremony in progress. The hole is usually eight inches in diameter and from eight to ten inches deep. The width of the rim should be one-tenth the diameter, and it should be one-tenth the width of the rim higher than the level of the ground under the eaves. The eaves area in Figure 140 is paved with concrete mixed with one-third part small stones. Paving the *chiriana* with the same mortar resulted in a pleasant feeling. The so-called peeping stone in the *chiriana* is a scenic touch. During a tea ceremony a pair of bamboo chopsticks are stuck into the hole. The usual length for chopsticks is 12 inches, and in this case we cut a joint like incision at a point about five inches up the stick then gradually sharpen to the end so that the end will be rounded.

The two-tiered stone in front of the wing wall, called the stone on which to place your swords, is a remnant of the times when the samurai really did have to remove their waist swords before entering the tea room. Now, of course, it is merely ornamental.

The row of stones in Figure 141 is called inset stones because they are set under the bottom of a house after the house has been built. They may be used as in the photograph, but small round stones set under the foundation or under the large beam that runs horizontally under the outside wall of a house also give a very elegant air. The height of the insets stones from the base under the eaves should be a little lower than the height of the stones on which the posts rest. They should usually show more than one inch from under the large foundation beam. There should be $\frac{3}{4}$-2 inches between the foundation stones and the inset stones, but the inset stones themselves should be as close together as possible and there tops sections should be flat and wide or the style will be unsuccessful. If the tops of the stones are narrow there will be unsightly openings between the individual stones.

Figure 140. Chiriana.

Figure 141. Inset stones.

PART THREE:
Planning and Constructions

CHAPTER ONE

Composite Plans

ALTHOUGH there is a great deal left to be said about auxiliary gardens, I intend to limit myself at this point to what I have already said about the most characteristic Japanese garden features. As a reference, however, I shall include here a number of examples of gardens in which these features have been combined for one home. Since, naturally, there are not many homes that would require all of the garden sections we have discussed, the gardens presented here are planned to meet the individual needs of the homes they accompany. There are examples of homes with rooftop gardens and of homes without them. There are instances in which there are tea gardens and instances in which there are none. There are even examples in which the fundamental front and kitchen gardens are missing. These, however, are exceptional cases when either the site is too small, or when the road on which the entrance faces is quiet enough that it is peaceful even without the separation a front garden provides.

§1   *Mr. S's Garden*

The Front Garden. As you see in Figure 142, this garden is divided into the fundamental sections (See Introduction, Chapter Two.), but since the roadway is 60 inches lower than the garden there is a staircase to the front entrance. The front garden (*Figure 143*) is higher than the remaining sections of the garden and is planted to seem deep to give a touch of quiet refinement to the bright house. A part of the front garden in the gate area (*Figure 144*) is left unplanted except for some small plants and *shichiku* bamboo and is spread with Sakuragawa gravel highlighted with a lantern and a *tsukubai*. In such a narrow space it is always safe to construct a refined gravel and bamboo garden.

The Kitchen Garden. The kitchen garden is merely a passageway between the rear gate and the kitchen door, but it provides storage space, laundry space, and together with the drying area on the roof, meets the needs of this type of equipment (*Figure 145*).

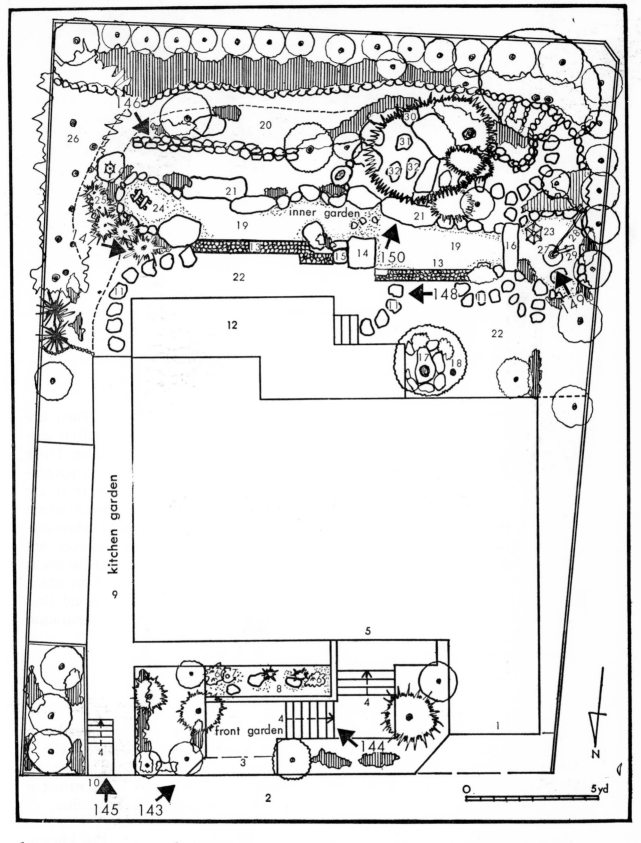

1	garage	9	passageway	17	water basin	25	cryptomeria
2	roadway	10	kitchen door	18	Japanese apricot	26	moso *bamboo*
3	gate	11	stepping stones	19	stream	27	water basin
4	staircase	12	veranda and terrace	20	sloping lawn	28	kakehi
5	front entrance	13	paving stones	21	stone arrangement	29	sozu kakehi
6	low bamboo	14	flat-top stones	22	lawn	30	waterfall
7	lantern	15	granite stones	23	Kasuga lantern	31	wave-dividing stone
8	Sakuragawa gravel	16	bridge	24	well	32	rapids

Figure 142. Plan of Mr. S's garden.

Figure 143. General view of Mr. S's front garden.

Figure 144. Detail of Mr. S's front garden.

Figure 145. Mr. S's kitchen garden.

The Inner Garden. The inner garden faces a combination Japanese-style veranda and Western-style terrace, which overlooks the garden from a level one step higher than the ground. Since the rear of the inner garden is high, it was very appropriate to make the terrace high. The stone-paved area in the garden is angled to harmonize with the line of the terrace-veranda and is paved completely in flag stones from the Tamba district. These light gray stones are relatively thin. There is also one large flat-top stone and some granite stones, that happened to be on hand, set into the pavement for variety.

Except the flagstones, all of the stones in the inner garden were on the site when the garden was being built. The bridge seen from the top of the constructed mountain in Figure 146, was also a piece of stone that was on hand and that looked as if it might make a good bridge. Though it is a little too thick, it serves the purpose well. The tall water basin in the corner of the veranda was also in the yard from the outset, but it has been set suitably and can be used for the tea ceremony. The planting is arranged for a heightened sense of perspective, with the slender Japanese apricot near the veranda as the foreground planting, the flowing wide belt of lawn as the middle ground, and the background planting as the distant ground.

We took advantage of the incline that faces the house (*Figure 147*) to arrange the stones so that the water that occasionally runs down here would form a waterfall. The stones are set in a natural stream-and-mountain arrangement which contrasts pleasantly with the straight lines of the paving stones.

The narrow flat strip of lawn is arranged so that it cannot be seen from the interior of the house because of the veranda railing. There is one flat space on the side of the slope to give a sense of ample room, and the remaining area slopes as much as possible and continues in grass to the bottom.

Because the stone Kasuga lantern, which was also on hand when we began, would not look good in a high place, we set it a level low so that it would seem to rise from the bottom of a stream. Water also flows in a stream from the well in the center of Figure 148. The *moso* bamboo planted against a background of cryptomeria is quiet and refined because it shields the garden from the neighboring houses. Had evergreens been used in place of the *moso* bamboo the refinement of the garden would have been lost, and the garden itself would have tended to seem narrower.

In front of the stone lantern (*Figure 149*) there is a steel-pot-shaped *tsukubai* with a *sozu kakehi* that tips up when the bottom pipe is filled with water. The stone over which the water flows in the

stone arrangement at the mouth of the waterfall (*Figure 150*) is a *tsukubai* that was in the garden all along and for which we had no other use. Because the quantity of water that crosses the fall is small, you can't see it in the picture, but it glitters when the sun or the moon shines on it. To make the arrangement seem to be a waterfall, even when there is no water falling from it, all of the stones incline steeply to the fall, and there is a wave-dividing stone in the fall basin. Whether the stones around the fall are standing straight or whether they are inclined, they look steep and contribute to the symbol of the force of the fall. Setting a stone straight or inclining it depends entirely on the nature of the stone. There are some stones that you might like to use standing straight, but cannot. On the other hand, the grain and shape of other stones make it imperative that they be used standing straight, or they will seem instable. In other words, it is important to activate the inherent nature of the stone. One of the stones on the left of the fall leans away from the falls, and as you can see, this arrangement, in which it also leans away from all the other stones, balances the strength of the setting. If the stone were turned so that it inclined to the right, all of the other stones would seem to be turned inside-out. A stone that naturally inclines in one direction is not something for people to willfully force

to incline in another. The people of old said that even the hearts of the coarse should not be forced, and it is also true that it is unforgivable to forcefully and willfully deprive a stone of its own natural beauty.

Figure 146. Mr. S's inner garden seen from the top of the artificially constructed hiflock.

There is a sort of rapids at the front of the fall basin and stepping stones in the pond for walking. Because the stones looked too conspicuous, we planted Japanese juniper and azaleas around them to make them look more refined.

Figure 147. West side of Mr. S's inner garden.

Figure 148. East side of Mr. S's inner garden.

Figure 149.   South side of Mr. S's inner garden.

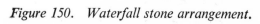

Figure 150.   Waterfall stone arrangement.

§2 *Mr. N's Garden*

The Front Garden. Figure 151 shows an over-all plan of the garden. Figure 152 shows the view of the main portion of the front garden from the front entrance gate. On either side of the pillars of the front gate, which are of Tsukuba stone, the same kind of stones in an uncut natural form are piled one on top another to form a wall 60 inches high and to add a considerable extension to the lot at the top. Planted on top are Japanese yew, azaleas, *asebo* and *dodan*, and *satsuki* planted among the boulders is flourishing and hides the stones to make them look more refined.

Because the handsome ferroconcrete house looked a little too splendid, we at first thought that planting large trees around it would give it a feeling of refinement and tried planting Chinese black pines, but the result was too extravagant and disagreed entirely with the feeling of the house. Removing some of the trees relieved the feeling of ostentation and made the garden seem more composed. The white object on the left in the photograph is a lighting fixture of forceful design.

The trough at the left of the top of the steps contains *hiiragi*-nandina, which is thriving to the point of overflowing the box. It was chosen for the trough because it can stand a lot of shade.

Figure 153 shows the area at the top of the stairs on the left of the front garden. Here and there in the Shirakawa gravel that is spread at the top of the steps are stepping stones that connect the house with the front staircase and that lead to the kitchen gate. The large azaleas planted on the right of the steps half conceal them and make them look refined. Concealing such a vital element as these stairs with trees has a refining effect and adds a touch of mystery that is characteristic of the Japanese garden.

Figure 154 shows the same section of the front garden from the top of the veranda stairs. Moss is planted under the black pines, at the edge of the stone embankment, and as a pathway to the service entrance. The moss was used because its color combines beautifully with the Shirakawa gravel. The flowers in the garden are designed to provide color all year round. For instance, the camellias bloom in the spring and in the fall, the *asebo* blooms early in the spring, and the azaleas in the early summer. In the late fall, the leaves of the *dodan* turn a beautiful red, and in the winter, the winter camellias are at their best. Because the lighting is poor from the steps to the entrance *tokusa*, *tsuwabuki* and ferns that can stand a lot of shade are planted there with one band of pondweed.

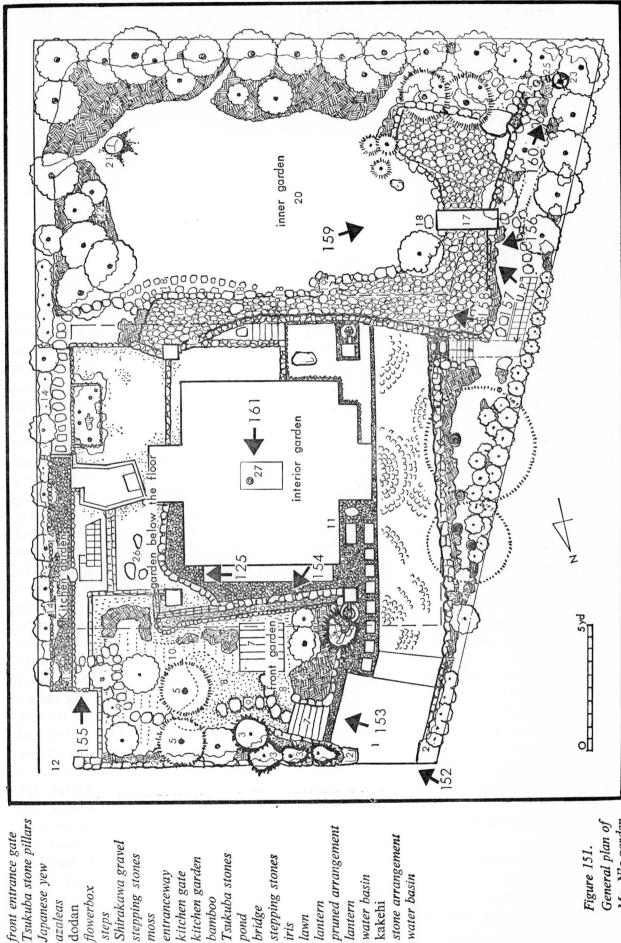

1 front entrance gate
2 Tsukuba stone pillars
3 Japanese yew
4 azaleas
5 dodan
6 flowerbox
7 steps
8 Shirakawa gravel
9 stepping stones
10 moss
11 entranceway
12 kitchen gate
13 kitchen garden
14 bamboo
15 Tsukuba stones
16 pond
17 bridge
18 stepping stones
19 iris
20 lawn
21 lantern
22 pruned arrangement
23 lantern
24 water basin
25 kakehi
26 stone arrangement
27 water basin

Figure 151.
General plan of
Mr. N's garden.

Figure 152. Exterior view of main section of Mr. N's front garden.

Figure 153. Front steps seen from front garden.

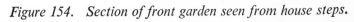

Figure 154. Section of front garden seen from house steps.

Figure 155. Mr. N's kitchen garden.

The Kitchen Garden. Since the floor of this house is high enough to accommodate the boiler, air-conditioning equipment, septic tank, and other machinery, and because there is also no need for a clothes drying area, the kitchen garden, in this case, need be only a passageway to the kitchen door. For this reason we were able to ornament and it beautify by planting *nari-hira* bamboo in the available margin of space. There was an excess space by the kitchen wall also in which to plant *moso* bamboo which not only serves to screen the house from the neighboring houses, but is beautiful as well. It is likely that this type of kitchen garden arrangement will be on the increase because of the recent developments in architectural design.

The Inner Garden. The inner garden pond, seen from the interior of the house in Figure 156, follows the line of the house and, on the far side, has a straight strip of Tsukuba stones arranged in a tortoise shell pattern. The bottom of the pond is paved with small round cobble stones from Ise. Bright colored carp add accent. The paving gives the feeling that when the pond is full of water all of the cobble stones are hidden, and when the water in the pond is low, a section of the stones are laid bare to form a stone beach. This, however, is only a mood, because what you see in the picture is the usual level of the water. Were the water of the pond to rise, it would overflow. This pond is designed to merely suggest changing water levels. A number of elements in Japanese gardens that seem simple but that conceal in themselves idea association content are also a part of the mysterious *shibusa*.

Figure 157 shows a section of the stone beach and a granite slab bridge crossing a curve in the pond. The edging stones we see in the preceding picture continue along here to form stepping stones to the bridge. In addition, these stones lead off from the front of the bridge to the thick planted small path in the inner section of the garden. Iris are planted along the pond edge only here and there so as not to destroy the general simplicity of the lawn and the pond edge. Since this garden gives a feeling of planned simplicity rather than of naturalness, it would have been out of place to design it as a field of iris. The lawn and the mountain-shape pruned shrubbery (*Figure 158*) are to the left of the arrangement in the preceding photograph. The lawn is the garden's middle ground and the pruned shrubbery is the distance. An earthenware lantern stands against the background of pruned shrubs in the upper right of the picture. Raising the ground level a bit and having the lawn shrubbery swell slightly saves the weakness of the lantern.

The entire pruned arrangement in the rear is trimmed to resemble a distant mountain. On the high section there are trident maple, ginkgo trees, camellia, *hiiragi*, and fragrant olive. In the mid-area there are reeves spiraea, *gaku*, evergreen burningbush, *kimmasaki*, *dodan*, *omura*, *kirishima*, Japanese quince, and *himemizuki*, whereas the low area contains daphne, *asebo*, azaleas, *satsuki*, and winter camellias. All year round either flowers blooming in succession or the red and yellow leaves of autumn, or the look of fresh greenery, give beauty to the garden. The *keyaki*, pasania, and Arabian jasmine on the left and the cherry, Japanese apricot, *kaido*, and pomegranate all rise from among the pruned shrubs and give the impression of trees planted upon a mountain. Although the pruned shrubbery is not yet finished, after a few years it will be fine.

In Figure 159 the camera has switched angles to show the right corner of the garden. In the deep greenery of the distance, a stone lantern peeps out. If one goes closer to the large stone standing fairly deep in water, he will see that the stone casts its reflection into the water. This section of the garden gives a feeling of seclusion and depth. The stone lantern is partially hidden to heighten the effect of a genuinely mysterious Japanese garden.

The large flat stone in the lawn in front serves as a table on which to drink tea or coffee, or as a sort of bench to sit on. This is a natural stone, only the top of which has been flattened and polished. This type of stone not only gives a free feeling of the open fields, but also adds a touch of elegant refinement.

Figure 160 shows a boulder-shaped water basin set at a spring near a stone lantern deep in the trees. A *kakehi* provides a supply of water. The water from this basin forms a small stream and flows into the pond. The stone lantern is called a *bonji* or sanskrit-character shape. Moss and fringed iris grow under the trees.

The Garden below the Floor. In this instance, the entrance is in a pilotis below the first floor, and we arranged three stones—a two-stone group and one separate stone for balance—in an area spread with Shirakawa gravel. There is a photograph of this garden in Part II, Chapter Two (*Figure 125*).

The Interior Garden. Although this looks like a courtyard garden, it is actually inside the house. A water basin stands in an area spread with blackish-purple Nachi gravel. Instead of putting the basin in the middle, we moved it over to the wall for the sake of spatial balance.

Figure 156. Inner garden pond seen from the house.

*Figure 157.
Pond with gravel beach
and stone bridge.*

Figure 158.   Lawn and mountain-shaped pruned shrubbery.

Figure 159.   Inner area of the lawn and shrubbery.

Figure 160. Boulder-shaped tsukubai *basin near a spring.*

Figure 161.   Interior garden.

Figure 162. Mr. F's front garden.

§3 *Mr. F's Garden*

The Front Garden. Figure 163 shows an over-all plan of the garden. The front garden plan is shown in Figures 162 and 164. Because this garden is spacious it was planted in camphor all over, except for a semicircular drive for the automobile, to shade and soften the ostentatious look of the house and to add refinement. The photograph was taken from the gate looking toward the entranceway. If one turned and looked in the other direction, he would see that the high trees in the garden shelter the house from the neighboring houses and create a very quiet environment.

The Kitchen Garden. Here again, because there is a storage room, a boiler, an entrance, and a domestic office entrance, the kitchen garden is only a passageway. The kitchen and the domestic office connect and face the inner garden, but the passageway most used for kitchen and domestic purposes is this kitchen garden (*Figure 165*).

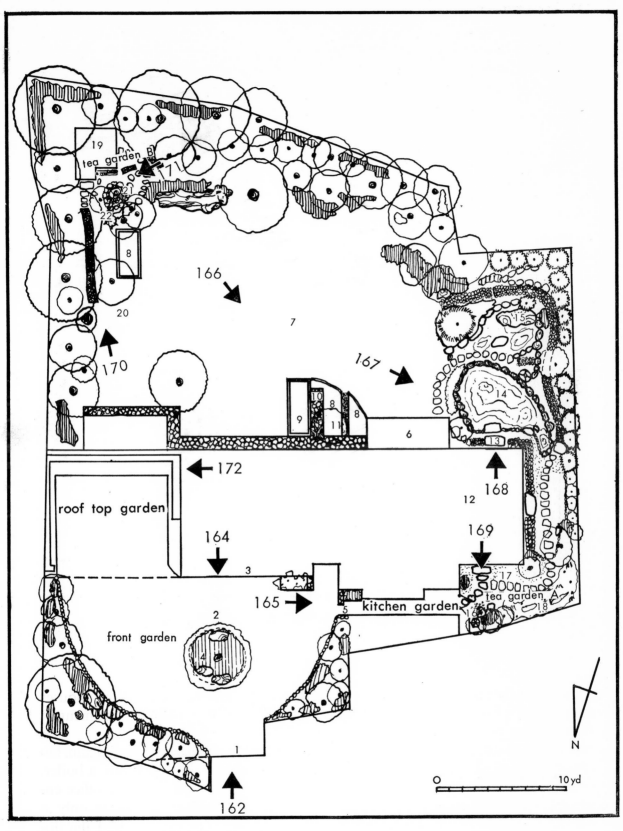

1	gate	7	lawn
2	semicircular drive	8	flowerbed
3	entranceway	9	pond
4	camphor	10	stone wall
5	passageway	11	crape myrtle
6	terrace	12	Japanese-style room

13	stone for the shoes	19	teahouse
14	pond	20	kitchen door
15	waterfall	21	tsukubai *water basin*
16	water basin	22	lantern
17	stepping stones		
18	moso *bamboo*		

Figure 163. General plan of Mr. F's garden.

Figure 164.
Mr. F's front garden seen from
the house entrance.

Figure 165.
Mr. F's kitchen garden.

The Inner Garden. As you can see in the plan, the inner garden, shut off from the noise and congestion of the road by the tall trees which surround it, is a very quiet area. In Figure 166, which was taken facing the house, we see that the garden is Western in style and features a lawn with a terrace jutting into it, flower beds, and a rectangular pond. The stone protective wall next to the pond was built to provide some relief in the mood created by the long unbroken lines of the building, by creating a partition that would separate the house into two sides. The crape myrtle behind the stone wall not only acts as an ornament to the house and relieves the harshness of its concrete surfaces with the softness of its leaves, but also provides cool shade. This arrangement as the foreground, the lawn as the middle ground, and the planting in the background work together to emphasize the sense of perspective. Because the garden level in front of the Japanese-style room was approximately the same as the level in front of the Western-style section of the house, to avoid the feeling of too little difference between the two, we cut away about eight inches of the ground in front of the Japanese-style room and set a stone for the shoes there. Both the Western-style terrace and the Japanese wooden veranda are very close to the level of the ground. When one sits in the Japanese manner on *tatami* in

the Japanese-style room, the atmosphere is unpleasantly humid.

There is a small pond in front of the Japanese-style room that has gently curving edges made of suitable stones arranged in a varying line. Few large stones were used in this border, and later the connecting concrete was completely concealed with still smaller stones. Using too many large stones would tend to make the pond look unrefined and ostentatious.

To set off the carp in the pond, the bottom was spread with refined, but whitish, granite stones about one to two inches in diameter. Though it is attractive just to spread the stones on the concrete pond bottom, cleaning them then becomes a great problem, because each stone would have to be removed separately. To solve this difficulty, these stones are spread on 1:1—1:2 mortar. If there are no interstices between the stones, they look almost as if they were merely sprinkled on top of the concrete. The tree in the right corner of the photograph is a maple and forms the foreground, the pond with its incidental greenery is the middle ground, and the waterfall and the green shrubbery is the background. All three combine to create a sense of perspective.

Figure 168, which shows the area around the waterfall in front of the Japanese room, is taken from the interior of that room. The large (13 tons) stone in the middle of the picture is an ashy stone from Kyoto. Because it has a concavity in its front surface, it was set naturally in a convex, concave fashion to form a waterfall. Although, in most cases, it is necessary to flank the middle stone, over which the water falls, with two narrow flanking stones, the feeling is simpler when one stone can serve the purpose of all three. When the amount of water in a fall is limited, the proper convexity and concavity is essential. This stone fits these conditions perfectly. When making a garden, if one comes across a stone like this one, he should be particularly careful to use it for a waterfall center stone.

Behind the waterfall are darkly rich trees like the cryptomeria, the pasania and the Japanese torreya. Maples overhang the fall, and rhododendron and *asebo* are planted at the bases of the stones. The large stone in the middle of the stream that flows from the fall to the pond is Kifune stone, as are the smaller stones on the bottom of the pond and the wave-dividing stone. Using one type of stone consistently is more composed and refined than mixing a number of different kinds. Kifune stones are of a darkish blue and purple, and the color combinations are gradual so that they do not look flashy. Sweet rush at the base of the stream stones and Dutch rushes at the bases of the larger stones dress up the water's edge.

Clumps of grasses form a connection between this Japanese-style garden and the Western-style lawn.

Figure 169 shows an enclosed tea garden seen from a Japanese-style room, which can be used for the tea ceremony because it has a hearth. The garden was designed to serve as a tea garden and contains a *tsukubai* with a *kakehi*. The basin is of the Roketsu type, whereas the stone lantern is an Oribe shape. There is a straw fence in the back with *kakuremino* planted against it. The stepping stones are weathered and refined Tsukuba stone, as are the edging stones around the "sea" of the *tsukubai*. Moss covers the ground, and *moso* bamboo grows on the left.

Figure 170 shows a view of the kitchen door of an independent *sukiya*, or detached teahouse, from the *roji*, which is in an inner section of a spacious lawn garden. The kitchen door of the teahouse is used by the host and his assistant during the tea ceremony. The paving stone are pure black small round stones from Kyoto, but it would also have been good to edge them with Tsukuba stones. To hide the kitchen door, we let the branchs of the trees grow and put undulations in the paved path. We worried a bit about how to make the two sides of the garden, the Japanese tea garden and the Western lawn garden, as different as possible. We decided to plant *otome* camellias on the side that faced the lawn and *hisakagi* on the side towards the tea garden. The garden gate at the *roji* makes the interior of the tea garden seem composed and refined.

Figure 171 shows the type of *tsukubai* arrangement we discussed earlier, in which the *tsukubai* is set one level down from the level of the garden so that one must descend to it to use the water. The basin is a natural boulder shape that is usually set on the other side of the stones that edge the "sea." In this case, however, it is just a little inward from the center of the "sea." The edging stones are grouped closely with Tsukuba stones for stability. The "sea" is spread with small Tsukuba stones, which are angular, a little stern looking, but appealing. Moreover, they take moss well, which makes them look more refined. As we mentioned before, it is usual to turn the mouth of the ladle to the left on a *tsukubai*, but since the cup of this ladle is shallow, it is also acceptable to turn it mouth up.

The lantern is of the *bonji*, or sanskrit-character, shape. If the same height ratio between the lantern and the height of the water is maintained, it is perfectly alright to use a lantern this tall. A lantern that is too large, or one with a cover with curved eaves, will not suit the *tsukubai*.

A Rooftop Garden. There is no view from the inner garden to the outside, but from the rooftop garden there is a distant view of Tokyo. On the other hand, between the city and the house there is a flat area with a lot of city streets. To hide these streets, we planted low shrubs at the edge of the roof. The narrow flat belt of lawn in front of the shrubbery has flowers planted in the middle. Because it was essential to put 20 inches of earth on the roof to plant the lawn and gardens, the garden level is higher than the level of the floor in front of the room. To solve this problem we built a retaining wall and a stone staircase. In one corner of the floor in front of the room there is a small pond. We also brought in and planted weeping willows which overhang to make a pleasant scene.

Figure 166. Section of inner garden seen from rear of garden.

Figure 167.   Pond in front of Japanese-style room.

Figure 168.   Waterfall seen from Japanese-style room.

Figure 169.   Closed-in tea garden.

Figure 170.
Tea garden's kitchen garden.

Figure 171. Tsukubai *setting.*

Figure 172. Rooftop garden.

§4 *Mr. T's Garden*

The Inner Garden. Because the entrance and the kitchen door look directly onto the streets, there is no front garden and no kitchen garden. Nevertheless, the feeling is one of composure and relaxation both because the street the house faces on is quiet and because the house is outstandingly well designed.

In a Japanese house the connections between the house and garden are usually from the floor of the house to the veranda, from the veranda to the shoe stone, and from the shoe stone to the ground. In a Western house they are from the floor of the house to the terrace and from the terrace to the garden. As you can see in Figure 174, which shows the area around this house, the veranda and the terrace have blended.

The stone for the shoes between the level of the ground and the level of the veranda provides a connecting link between the garden and the house. The area under the eaves is covered in gravel and has a border of small stones. This is perhaps not in keeping with the modern mood of the architecture, but as you can see, the design seems uncrowded. There is a stream of water between the *moso* bamboo on the left and the lawn. The eulalia and the bush clover suggest the elegance of the ancient flower and tree gardens. The winter daphne and azaleas under the bamboo are not suitable and should be replaced with plants that thrive in the shade like the *kakuremino*, the spear flower, and the *tachi-bana*. The lawn with no path and no stepping stones creates a fresh effect. The large stone in the inner section near the veranda would look more composed if it were set deeper so that its base entered the ground.

The high pruned Chinese black pine hedge on the right in Figure 175, which is the view from the opposite end of the garden, helps balance the two-story house. It not only shields the house from neighboring houses, but also gives the garden a neat atmosphere. The stones in the rear seem to be in disorder now, but when the base plants and grasses grow, they will look better. The sharp pointed evergreens at the end of the garden make the garden seem larger and that section more distant. If, on the other hand, they had been rounded deciduous trees, the inner side would have seemed closer and the garden shallower. The weeping willow on the right is strikingly different from the other trees because of the angle of its branches and makes a charming accessory to the rest of the garden.

Figure 176 shows the hedge and the stepping stones, which are a continuation on the right of the scene in the preceding photograph. The hedge and the upper section of the house form two horizontal lines, and the stepping stones a third. Because there is nothing in front of these stepping stones except a flat lawn the garden here has a simple feeling.

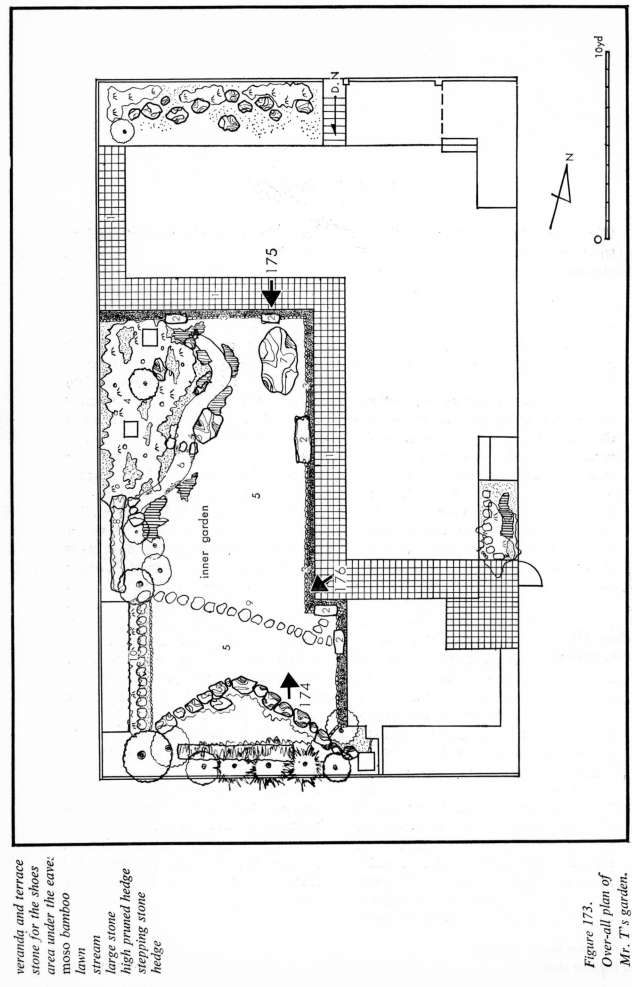

1 veranda and terrace
2 stone for the shoes
3 area under the eaves
4 moso bamboo
5 lawn
6 stream
7 large stone
8 high pruned hedge
9 stepping stone
10 hedge

Figure 173.
Over-all plan of
Mr. T's garden.

Figure 174.
Inner garden area near house.

Figure 175.
Far section of inner garden.

Figure 176.
Inner garden lawn with hedge
and stepping stones.

CHAPTER TWO

Construction Points

§1 *Pond Construction*

IF YOU are building a pond in an area with high underground water so that you can use a natural spring as a water source, determine the average depth of the water below the surface of the ground, and then decide on the water level and depth of the pond you want. Next lay out the shape of the pond with a rope, and erect batten boards for measurement reference. Using these levels as a standard, begin digging the pond. Dig the hole deeper than the scheduled depth of the pond and keep a pump pumping throughout the construction so that standing water will not be a nuisance. If the place has good drainage, lay a drain pipe at the very beginning to keep the water drained off.

At the spots where stones are to be set, drive pine or concrete pilings into the ground and cover them with a layer of concrete four inches thick, when the concrete has dried, the stones can rest on these poles.

If you are going to make a grassy bank instead of a stone one, carve away the sides to more than a thirty-degree angle, and plant sweet rushes, low strip-ed bamboo, and other grasses that grow well in the water.

Even though the underground water is at a distance, if you can use it freely in your pond, eliminate only the step in which you let in the water, and follow the same procedural order as above. Set the stones, lay a layer of concrete on the pond bottom, and fill in the cracks between the stones only below the water surface.

If you must rely on city water or on your own private water supply, you must be careful to build the pond in such a way as to absolutely guard against leakage. First plan just as above, erect batten boards, estimate the water level, decide on the pond's depth, lay a water drainage pipe, then begin digging the pond's outline. Have the bottom incline at about a 1/80 or 1 inch drop to 80 inches, toward the drainage pipe. Cover the bottom with a layer of stones roughly four inches in diameter or with four inches of concrete. Pack it in firmly. Put in the fine packing gravel and rough concrete mixed to one part concrete, three parts river sand, and six parts gravel the bottom where the sides of the wall will rise. This concrete should be approximately twelve inches wide and four inches thick.

On top of this will go the pond walls, usually concrete about four inches thick with all tops horizontal. The walls are of a 1:3:6-proportion cement. Usually the pond walls are about twelve inches tall. It is better to have the walls incline about one inch back at the top to prevent the expanding ice in the winter from cracking the concrete. In this case, since the concrete is built up from the bottom, you would not need a temporary framework. You only need one when the walls of the pond are to be perpendicular to the bottom of the pond. After you have poured the concrete for the walls, let it set for two or three days, then remove the framework, and pour the concrete for the bottom. This should be of the same proportions as the concrete mentioned above and should be poured in a four-inch layer. If you do not use a framework, pour the bottom concrete right after you have poured the walls. When you have poured the concrete, cover it in a $\frac{1}{4}$–$\frac{1}{2}$-inch layer of a mixture of one part cement and two parts river sand as quickly as possible. Storing water will not be a problem if you do this. If the weather is not cold enough to freeze wait three to five days till the concrete is firmly set and begin the stone arranging.

If the pond is only 50–60 square yards, reinforcements in the concrete are unnecessary, but if the pond is larger, you should use $\frac{1}{2}$ inch steel reinforcing rods at a twelve-inch interval or $\frac{1}{4}$ inch rods at a six-inch interval, and the concrete should be six inches thick. On the other hand, the foundation is the prime feature, and if it is bad, the reinforcements and the thicker concrete will not prevent the pond from cracking. Examples of completely undamaged ponds of 300 square yards built 30 years ago with only four inches concrete walls and no reinforcements indicate that if the foundation is good, steel reinforcements may not be necessary. In addition, if you use sifted sand with no impurities in a one-to-two proportion with mortar, the pond will not leak even if you do not use waterproofing materials.

In pouring the concrete for the pond, take care to lay some crushed concrete before pouring the side walls, and in the cases of square or rectangular ponds, give the corners a rounding off by coating them with mortar. You can get a very nice round-corner finish using

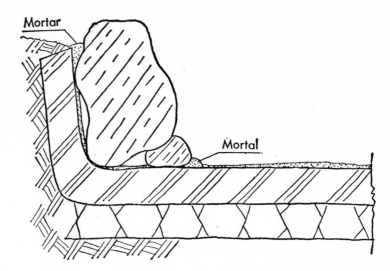

Figure 177. Cross section of pond concrete wall and stone arrangement.

something like a cylindrical bottle. If you are not careful with this, the corners may crack. In addition, in the finishing mortar, attempt to use as clean and evenly sifted sand as possible. A fine-sand grain of from $\frac{1}{10}$ to $\frac{1}{8}$ inch is good.

Because this one-to-two mortar mixture will crack easily if it is in too much sun, spray the concrete with a watering can or a hose, and keep it covered with straw mats for about two days to prevent it from drying too quickly.

In the case of a small pond of from 10 to 20 square yards, if the stones are hard and have a fine grain so that they will not absorb water, place the bank and center stones in the proper stone arrangements, then pour the concrete, and the pond will not leak. When you have poured the concrete, paint the joints between the stones and the concrete with a thin mixture of water and cement, applying it with a paint brush. This will bind the concrete to the stone surfaces and will prevent water leakage. This method is also used on old concrete and stones to close off the small invisible air particles in the concrete.

Pond construction is difficult because stones cannot be buried in set concrete. Since there is no way out of this situation, when you must bury the bases of a large number of stones, you will have to dig depressions for them and line the depressions with concrete. Fortunately, these instances are rare. If, on the other hand, in a pond of a depth of twelve inches, you have unnecessary spaces in which you would like to sink some stones, if the stones are too low, first sink another stone to act as a base for the one you want to show, then place the latter stone on top of the base stone.

There are often openings between the set stones and the concrete walls of the pond through which both dirt and mud will fall. To prevent this, in cases where the opening is not large enough to fill with a stone or concrete slab, press the stones in well, and fill in all the upper surface openings with a one-to-three mixture of mortar. The openings at the bottoms of the stones should be filled in also, as you see in Figure 177, because this will prevent them from sliding in the case of an earthquake. Also coat the stone and mortar slabs you have inserted between the larger stones and the concrete with mortar to keep them from moving and to improve their appearance. Because these stones are in the water, when they become dirty, their colors will be inconspicuous.

The water will look lovelier in the

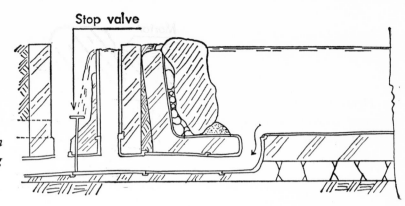

Figure 178. Cross section of water drainage opening from pond bottom.

pond if you put some round small stones on the bottom and fix them firmly with mortar so that when the pond is being cleaned they can be easily scrubbed with a brush without being removed from the pond.

If you intend to use carp or large gold fish in your pond, you must make the depth of the pond greater than the length of the full-grown fish. You may, however, have only one section, say an area of about four square yards, that is 40 inches deep and leave the remaining sections of the pond twelve inches in depth. If you put small round stones or gravel at the shallow end of the pond, the water and the fish themselves will be more beautiful.

Usually the spillway and drainage opening are on a side of the pond that is from $\frac{3}{4}$ to 1 inch lower than the other walls. There is a compartment behind the wall to catch the water from the spillway and from the drainage opening at the bottom of the pond. Build

the overflow at the opposite end of the pond from the supply inlet to create better water circulation. In Figure 178 you can see that the application of a syphon principle means that the constant circulation of the water from the bottom of the pond to the top and out the overflow keeps the water clear.

For reference as to the amount of materials and labor required for a pond approximately one square yard in size, we offer the following table in which the concrete is taken to be four inches thick and the mortar $\frac{1}{3}$ inch thick. Multiply these thicknesses by the area of the bottom and the walls of the pond, and you can calculate how much concrete and how much labor will be needed. You can also calculate these in the case of thicker concrete by doubling the figures.

In the case of a concrete pond, let water into it, let the water stand for about a month, let this water out, refill with fresh water, and then put in a number of fish. Although letting the

Concrete and Labor Chart for a Pond Approximately One Yard Square

(Concrete—four inches thick, mortar, $\frac{1}{3}$ inch thick)

operation / items	proportions	cement	river sand	gravel	broken stone	labor
concrete	1:3:6	0.45 bags	0.05 m³	0.094 m³		0.3 man
mortar	1:2	0.15 bags	0.01 m³			0.1 man
digging						0.2 man
pebble setting					0.1 m³	0.05 man
covering mud (40″)						0.1 man
total		0.6 bags	0.06 m³	0.094 m³	0.1 m³	0.75 man

Figure 179. Laying out the stream's shape.

sun shine on a mortar finished pond for two or three days will quickly neutralize the surface, it may also harm the water retaining capacity of the pond. In this case, too, it is safer to put water in first and let it stand. When you let the water out, clean the mortar with a brush, then refill with fresh water. After this water has stood for a few days, you may put in the fish.

§2   Stream Construction

If water is abundant, you may just let it flow, and any type of stones at all will set it off well. On the other hand, since gardens with such abundant water supplies are very scarce, it is a question of some labor and effort to create a stream that will give the feeling of composed movement on the surface of the water and the gentle murmuring of a stream, where there is only a small amount of water available. In the case of a small supply of water, the incline should be about 1/80, or a 1 inch drop to 80-inches.

First lay out a rope to estimate the shape of the stream, then determine whether the stream is to be seen from close up or from a distance. When you have decided where the curves in the stream are to be, drive poles, one on each side of the stream outline like those in Figure 179, then make a mark for the ground line at the same height on all of the poles. Measure the distances between all of the poles, beginning with the pole farthest upstream, then sink the first two pole to a position where their tops are at the same height as the ground line you established before, and nail a brace between them at that spot. Proceed to the second set of poles and lower their tops so that they provide a drop of $\frac{1}{2}$ inch to 40 inches from the first poles and drive them in on either side of the stream. Continue to the third set of poles, and repeat the same process, always nailing a brace at the proper height between the poles. Establish the height of the surface of the stream water at pole one, taking the pattern of the garden and the height of the ground through which the stream must pass into consideration.

When you have decided on the water level, take into consideration the depth of the water, the thickness of the layer of gravel, the thickness of the mortar and concrete, and the thickness of the broken stone foundation, and you can decide on the depth to which you must cut. Cut a stick to this length with which you can measure from the brace nailed to the two poles (see *Figure 180* and note number A). Stretch a string from brace

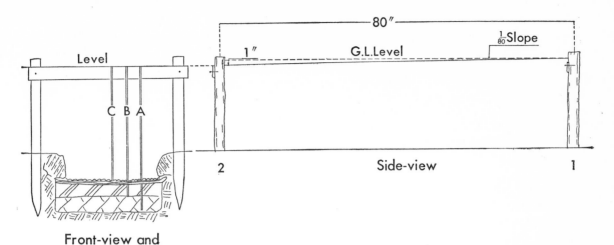

Front-view and cross section *Figure 180.   Cross section of stream under construction.*

to brace all along the line of the stream, and measuring with the pole from the string, you will always know how deep to dig the stream bed.

When you have finished digging the stream bed, shorten the measuring stick by the thickness of the foundation layer of broken stone (*Figure 180*, B) and using the shortened stick as a measure lay the proper thickness of broken stone throughout the length of the stream. On top of the crushed stone spread a layer of fine gravel and pack it thoroughly into all the nooks and crannies. Packing the gravel down firmly fills up the soft places in the ground and makes for more standardized measurements.

Next, shorten the measuring stick by the thickness of the layer of concrete you are going to lay (*Figure 180*, C), and pour the concrete to the depth the measuring stick indicates. Then finish the concrete with a coating of mortar.

If, because of the scenery or because of the level of the land, you cannot have an incline of 1/80, it is good to have the pool eddy here and there. You can construct eddies by simply not inclining the bottom of the stream and by increasing the depth at given spots.

Usually, when the supply of water is small, the water will be about $\frac{3}{4}$ to 1 inch deep, the gravel will be about the same, the mortar will be $\frac{1}{2}$ inch thick, the concrete from $2\frac{1}{2}$ to 4 inches, and the crushed stone four inches. If you spread the bottom of a stream that is only $\frac{3}{4}$ or 1 inch deep with gravel that is about $\frac{3}{4}$ inch in diameter, the friction of the flowing water against the stones will set up a murmuring sound. This is not a loud clamourous noise, of course, but is a refined and leisurely sound of the wavelets the stream makes as it flows along.

If the incline of the stream is steep and the amount of water small, the water will flow under the gravel on the bottom and will not be visible. In such cases, it is best to attach the gravel to the bottom of the stream with mortar. Although setting each piece of stone individually in the mortar is tedious work, if you merely sprinkle the gravel on the mortar, more of the mortar than of the gravel will show, and this is distasteful. On the other hand, it might turn out that the gravel would sink too deep in the mortar so that the stream would not make a murmuring sound. All in all, there is no way out of setting each piece of stone individually in the mortar so that there are no openings of any size between the stones. In doing this, the proper grading of the gravel is important, because ungraded gravel looks messy. The gravel should be larger than one inch in diameter. If the gravel is set in mortar, it is easy to clean with a long-handled brush.

Although in the case of a pond, the stones are not set until after the concrete is poured, because the water pressure in a stream is low, you may set the stones, then pour the concrete. This makes the stream much easier to construct.

To give the line of your stream gentle curves, arrange stones larger than four inches in inconspicuous ins and outs, and partially conceal them with mosses and rushes. You might also line the edges of the stream with small round stones, but because if you set these stones and then pour the concrete they will move easily, it is best to pour the concrete first, then set the small stones in as you are laying the mortar.

This is the complete process, from beginning to end, of making a simple stream, but of course, if you are going to use rapids or falls in the stream the digging and the laying of the concrete will vary appropriately.

As we have said, the low water pressure in a shallow stream makes it possible to pour the concrete after setting the stones in their arrangements; however, in the case of eddies where the water will be deeper, pour the concrete and add the finishing mortar before setting the stones, just as you would in a pond.

§3   *Setting the Pagoda and the Stone Lantern*

There are a great many types of pagodas, but the ones we use in the garden are the 13-, 12-, 9-, 7-, and 5-story ones, or the ones that emphasize the projecting eaves. In one pagoda, perhaps only one eave will be unusually large, as in the Hannya-ji pagoda, or the eaves may be staggered one large to one small as in the Yakushi-ji pagoda. The Hokke-in pagoda, the *gorin* pagoda, the treasure tower, the *niju-hasshuku* pagoda, and many others, should be set in a place designated for some commemorative purpose, on a high place, in the middle of a mountain slope, in a spot hidden by trees, or in a place that overlooks the water.

These pagodas were originally used in the Buddhist faith as memorial towers or as relic towers, but once they became an object to be used in the garden for their visual merits alone, they also became nothing more than a fine piece of the stonecutter's art. The owner of a

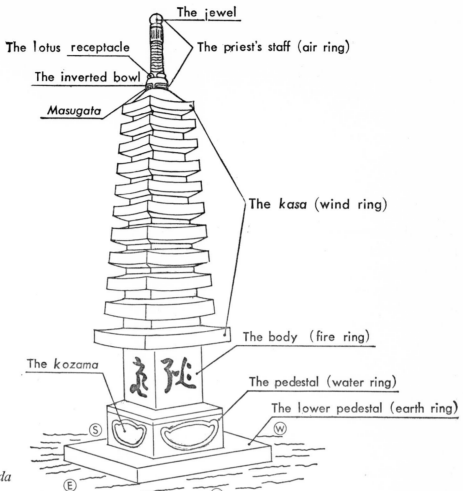

The jewel

The priest's staff (air ring)

The lotus receptacle

The inverted bowl

Masugata

The *kasa* (wind ring)

The *kozama*

The body (fire ring)

The pedestal (water ring)

The lower pedestal (earth ring)

Figure 181.
Parts of a pagoda
(*eleven stories*).

garden may take the original meaning of these towers into consideration if he likes, or he may not, depending on his personal tastes and on the needs of the garden plan.

The way you face the pagoda, depends on the garden, but we do not ordinarily face them straight forward. It is better to turn them slightly so that two sides show at once and give a sense of dimension (*Figure 181*).

It is more convenient to explain the pagoda if we first explain the names of each of its parts.

Starting from the top of the eleven-story pagoda in Figure 180, we see the long slender staff-like finial with the round jewel at the top; this is the so-called priest's-staff jewel and is known as the *air ring* of the tower. Depending on the type of pagoda, the next section may consist of a number of eave-like projections called *kasa*; this section is known as the *wind ring*. The section that begins where the *kasa* of the *wind ring* end is known as the trunk or the *fire ring*. In the three and five-story treasure towers, where there are the same number of lamp compartments as there are stories, these compartments correspond to the trunk in an ordinary pagoda. Beneath the trunk is the *water ring*, and beneath that is the *earth ring*. There are pagodas with a one- or two-step foundation-like

Figure 182.   Symbol for east.

pedestal beneath the earth ring, but these pedestals fall outside of the list of earth, water, fire, wind, and air rings, which a proper five-ring tower must have. Any tower that is not a five-ring tower need not necessarily adhere to this arrangement. The lotus-shaped section that holds the upper section of the finial is called the *juge*, the section beneath that shaped like an inverted pot is called the *fusebachi*, and the section below that, square in this case, but hexagonal in the case of a hexagonal pagoda, is called the *masugata*. As you can see in the diagram, there is an area carved out in the water ring; this area is called the *kozama*.

The trunk and the *masugata* of the air ring indicate the direction in which the pagoda is turned. The character in Figure 182 is read *mun* and indicates east. This character is carved on the trunk of the pagoda, but it is not always necessery to have it face true east. However, if you move the *mun* from true east to suit the needs of the garden or for a nicer appearance, naturally all of the other signs indicating north, west, and south, will be out of line also. In the bottom section of Figure 181 the points of the compass are indicated, and carved on the trunk of the pagoda are the characters *mun*, which, as we have said, indicates east, and *aku* which indicates north.

There are also pagodas with four gods carved on the trunk. Of these four, the easiest to recognize is the turtle. Turn the turtle to the north and the red bird carving will face the south, the blue dragon will face the east, and the white tiger, the west.

Because the word *nijuhasshuku*, in the name of the *nijuhasshuku* pagoda, means the twenty eight solar stages along the zodiac, this tower naturally has connections with the four directions. The four gods, the turtle, the red bird, the blue tiger, and the white dragon are each assigned seven of the solar stages. In setting the pagoda, if you set it so that, for instance, the blue dragon faces east, the solar stages on the pagoda will be correct. This is an unusual lantern, and I have only had one occasion to set one of them.

Because on the pagodas with Buddhist carvings, the Buddha with his hands held palms up above his lap, represents Amida Buddha he should be set facing west. The carvings on the cheaper pagodas all show Bhudda in the same manifestion, and it makes no difference which way you face the tower. If you understand this much about setting the pagoda, even if there is no clear indication in the garden plans, your settings will be correct.

To prevent the pagodas falling over in an earthquake or any terrific ground tremor, pierce the center from top to bottom with a brace.

In front of a stone lantern there is a flat front stone to step on when lighting the lantern. This, however, is not its only function. Because it also serves as a horizontal contrast to the verticality of the lantern, it is not really necessary to set this front stone high enough for a person to be able to put his hand in the light compartment of the lantern if the lantern itself is very tall. When the lantern is small, the contrast between the low broad front stone and the towering lantern, becomes the front stone's only purpose. With the same idea of contrast in mind, we put a large front stone before a tall pagoda to set it off to good advantage. If you want the stone to look close to the pagoda, separate the two only by about eight to twelve inches. If you want the stone to look 50 or 100 yards away from the pagoda, set them one yard, or several yards apart. There are even cases in which the front stone is on the near side of a pond and the pagoda itself on the far side.

Although the relationship between the planting and the pagoda is clearly indicated in the plans for a garden, since it is better to have an understanding of how this should be done when you are actually constructing a garden, we shall discuss it now.

Because deciduous trees usually tend to be rounded and to create a mood of gloom, to emphasize the loftiness of the pagoda it is better to plant around it such evergreens trees that rise tall and straight as the Japanese torreya, the momi fir, the Japanese white pine, the Japanese yew, the cryptomeria, the cypress, or sawara cypress.

Since there is no reason to attempt to make low pagodas symbolize loftiness, it is fine to use rounded deciduous trees, some of the curving pines, or some of the maples around them. It is also good to have the pagoda stand in some shrubbery if there are no tall standing trees near by. This is an example of substituting a feeling of close intimacy for that of loftiness.

Put lights in the light compartments of the three- and five-story pagodas, and plant double cherries, pink cherries, or white cherries around them for a gorgeous sight when the flowers bloom. There is also a very special feeling about this type of pagoda reflecting in water on a spring night.

A light is the very life of a stone lantern, and you can tell the front of a lantern by the large unobstructed opening to the light compartment. You need, not, however, always set this front side directly facing into the garden. Doing so is something like taking a photograph of a married couple or of some friends in which both people stare directly into the camera. Nothing could be less indicative of intimacy or love than this pose; it seems to suggest more that there is some sort of fight going on between the two. Having the wife turn slightly towards the husband, on the other hand, introduces a feeling of emotional warmth to the picture. In much the same way setting a lantern a little to the right of center in the garden and having it face slightly to the left gives a feeling of intimate unity between the lantern and everything else in the garden. This is what we mean by saying, "setting things in accordance with the needs and will of the garden." Of course, if you are using the lantern to light the water basin, the entrance to the garden, or the garden path you should have the lamp face the area it is to light; nevertheless, even in these cases, it does not do to forget what we have just said about setting things in the garden to give it the flavor of intimacy and to suit the garden's own personality. Although, if the lantern is carved, the moon on it usually faces west and the star east, here again, the feeling and personality of the garden should have pre-eminence.

You should put the lattices in the lamp opening at night and take them out in the daytime, unless the lamp is electrically lit, in which case, do not take the lattices out, because if you do the light bulb inside will show.

To set either the pagoda or the lantern dig and pack down a hole about four inches deep, pour in some rubble or concrete chips, and pack that down.

On top of this pour in some fine gravel and pack this down. Using your own judgement, set the lantern or pagoda so that the foot of the earth ring is more than three to four inches lower than the packed level of the garden ground. If you are setting a large lantern or pagoda of more than seven yards, pour a layer of concrete eight inches thick on top of this. To do this you must first dig a fairly deep hole. Figure 183 shows the names of each of the parts of the stone lantern. As you can see, beginning at the top there are the jewel, the cover, the light compartment, the central platform, the post, and the earth ring (or the pedestal stone). There are lanterns that are carved from one solid piece of stone, and there are others that are made up of two or three stones set together. Though the part names are all the same, there are types like the Michi-shirube lantern in which there is no cover and no central platform and the light compartment and the post are joined directly. As you can see in the preceding photographs, they are stone lanterns without earth rings. There is also an extreme type, called the Shingen lantern, in which even though there is a light compartment there is no place to put a light.

When you have completed the foundation for the stone lantern, if the lantern is small, say under two yards in height, take a horizontal sighting, and

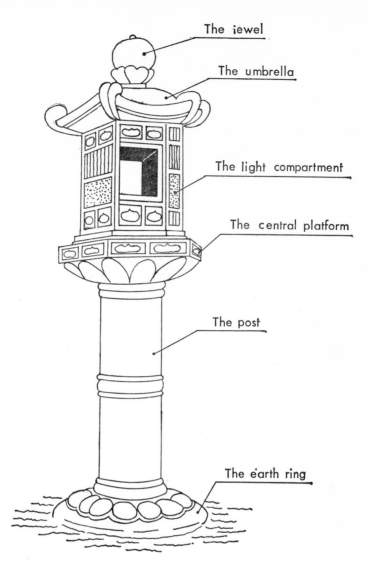

The jewel

The umbrella

The light compartment

The central platform

The post

The earth ring

Figure 183.
Parts of a stone lantern
(Todai-ji Sangatsudo *shape*)

set the earth ring level, then add the remaining sections in proper order: the post, the central platform, the light compartment, the cover, and the jewel. If you are setting a lantern that is too tall for you to reach arrange a temporary platform near the lantern, and set the cover before you set the light compartment. Get up on the platform, get someone to put the light compartment on top of the post while you hold the cover up, then place the cover on top of the light compartment and adjust the setting.

Because all of the parts in some lanterns are somewhat distorted, use a level

to set all of the sections to the light compartment, and set the remaining sections perpendicular with a plumb. In addition many lanterns will tend to shake a little, so put in some sand in any place where you think there might be a crack or an opening between the sections. If the lantern you are setting is too large to be handled by hand, use a crane or set up a fork supported on both sides with cables, and use a winch and a block at the same time. Let the supporting cables slack a little and incline the fork directly over the position of the lantern, then let the block go slack and lower it. Be careful that the

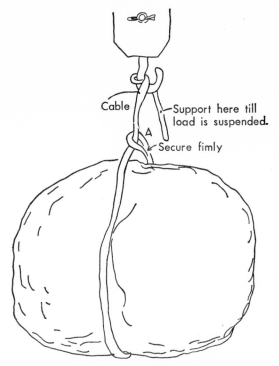

Figure 184. Suspending a stone on a pulley.

cables used to incline the fork and the supporting and winding equipment are safe and secure. If you then apply a winch to this set-up, you can set the lantern comfortably.

When using ropes, chains, or wires to move the light compartment of a lantern, never run them through the holes in the lantern. Moreover, when you are transporting the light compartment, never run poles or anything of the sort through the holes in the compartment, because though the stone is hard, it may break. Always wrap the trunk of the light compartment with two or more layers of rope, then attach another rope to the first one and use the second rope to suspend the light compartment. Tighten the first rope well. When using cables or chains to move these stone objects, it is important to wrap them either in cloth or in rush matting to prevent the stone surfaces from being scratched. Particularly with old lanterns, it takes a considerable time for the scratches to heal to the lantern's original condition.

When you are going to transport a lantern or pagoda, first check to see if there were any mistakes in the original setting. If the setting is correct, move around to the rear of the lantern, and make guide marks at the places where the various sections join. Later, after you have moved the lantern, you can reset it using the guide marks you made to show you how the pieces should fit together. When you have set a pagoda or a lantern, and the front stone is in place, sweep away the dirt and dust and sprinkle the entire setting with water to encourage the development of a pleasant patina and the growth of moss.

§4 *Stone Arrangement Construction*

The surface of a stone shows its anti- quity and refinement. If it is covered with moss and if the softer feldspar and mica sections have weathered away leav- ing the harder quartz sections to stand out, it is easy to see that the stone has passed through many ages. For this rea- son, when moving or taking a stone from the ground, be particularly careful not to damage its surface. Use a crowbar on only the back side or on the bottom of the stones, and if you must use a lever after the stone has been set, use a wooden one. When stones will be coming into contact with other stones, with chains or with cables, be sure to pad them with soft cloth, straw mats, or scrap lumber. If it is a particularly fine stone, it is im- portant enough to warrant being padded with an old cushion or pillow. Once the surface of a stone has been scratched it takes many years for it to recover its original appearance.

When setting stones in the ground, measure the depth of the root, and dig a hole to that depth. Pack the soil in the hole down well, then after packing it again with a pole that is from $2\frac{1}{2}$ to 4 inches in diameter, put in the stone. The root of the stone is the part that is below the ground level line in the first drawing in Figure 185. This stone

setting, called cutting the root, shows in a glance what the size of the stone is. It is never good to set stones so that they look small. It is usual to set stones so that they look as if they are rising up out of the ground and shoving their tops upward from the very bowels of the earth. A wide bottomed stone with the bottom cut off like the one in number two of Figure 185, should be set only slightly into the ground. Though most stones are better set deep, there is no need to set them unreasonably deep in cases like this. There are instances, like that in number three of Figure 185, when we set stones in a river or some other body of water, and we do not think of burying the stone's root at all. This type of setting is called "dependent stones," and expresses the lively move- ment of the stones, the dancing of the waters, and the shifting of stones. Because this setting must give a feeling of the base stone's firmly supporting and holding the other stones, the setting must be stable both horizontally and vertically.

The upper side of a stone is the side with no scars on its surfaces and which if set as the upper surface will make the stone seem larger. Stones that project to the right or left have the projecting side

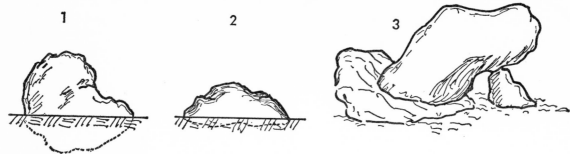

Figure 185. Setting the bases of stones.

as their front. Sometimes these stones are set to lean backwards to seem to be responding to some other stone. If a stone has a vertical shape or grain, set it vertically. If it has a flat top, set it so that the top is horizontal and level. If a large stone has a shelf-like flat section, set the stone so that the shelf is horizontal and level to give the stone character and a feeling of stability. If you have a stone whose shape does not indicate any particular setting, choose a part that looks somewhat flat, make that part the top, and set it level so as to make at least something out of the stone.

If you have decided to express the full use of the energetic spirit of the stones, put in small support stones under the bottom of the large stone where the largest area comes in contact with the ground. Do not let these small stones jut out farther than the large stone. Pack the ground down with a small pole, then fill in the hole with earth to the ground level. After the stones are set, clean away the dust and dirt that hinder the development of a patina and the growth of moss, and at the end of the day sprinkle the stones with a watering can or with a sprinkler.

Even a setting of just one stone is a stone group that will combine with something. The stone may not have a companion stone, but if its force is directed toward the left to the garden, it combines with the garden spaces. It may combine with a group of trees or with a body of water, or with a building. If the stone has absolutely no connection with anything at all, it cannot be called a stone group.

In cases where two or more stones are combined, they may be grouped in a side-to-side relationship or in a vertical relationship. When we say a stone group, we do not necessarily mean that the stones must come into actual physical contact. Though there are instances in which the stones are separated by from one to four inches, there are also others in which they are separated by as much as 100 yards. Both are stone groups.

When the stones are in a side-to-side relationship it is possible to have one stone supporting the other. In these cases you may set the support stone first, then set the stone that is to be supported. On the other hand, if the stone that is to be supported is larger and heavier than the support stone, first determine the facing and the position of the stone that is to be supported and fix it with chain and block so that it will not fall over. When this is done,

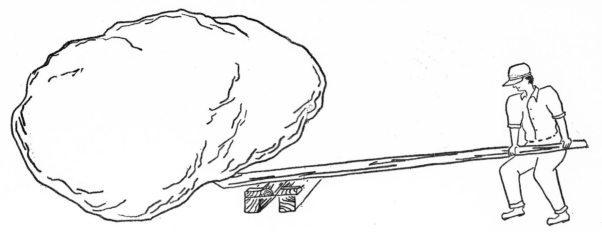

Figure 186.   Lever and fulcrum.

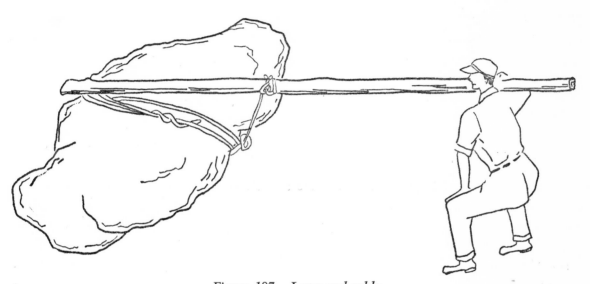

Figure 187.   Lever and cable.

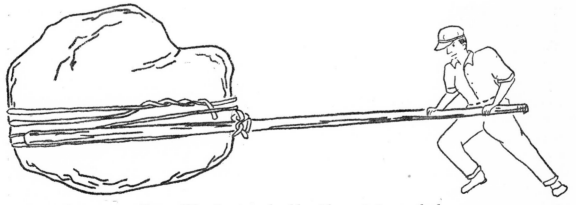

Figure 188.   Lever and cable with a rotating method.

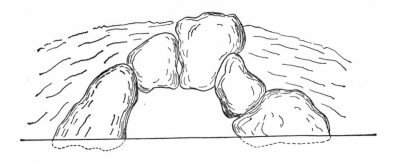

Stress directed from top to bottom

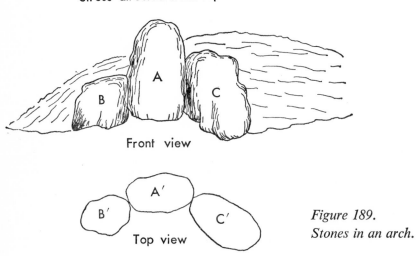

Front view

Top view

Figure 189.
Stones in an arch.

Stress directed from the rear forward

set the smaller column-like support stone, then lower the larger stone onto it.

When you are setting one or more stones, that weigh over 110 pounds, you will be better able to set it as you want, if you use a block or a winch. It is difficult to get the stone set the way you have in mind using only a lever. Moreover, the lever method requires much more time than you might think. You can, however, easily set some stones using levers, particularly when there are too few to make using machinery worthwhile. For the sake of reference, I will mention a few of the lever methods we use to move two or three stones. There is the usual spring-board lever method (*Figure 186*), the rolling stone method (*Figure 187*), and the revolving stone

method (*Figure 188*). These are all done as they are shown in the charts. There is an additional method in which no special fulcrum block is used and one end of the lever is shoved under the stone and the other end used to lift up.

When you are going to suspend a stone in the process of setting it, estimate the stone's center of gravity, and attach the cable surrounding the stone to the chain block as shown in Figure 184. Secure the cable either with your hand or by holding it in place with a thin rope until the stone begins to move. If the stone must be lifted to any height, it is much safer to secure the cable with shackles.

When arranging stones in tiers, you must think first of the principles of leverage and of the arch so that the

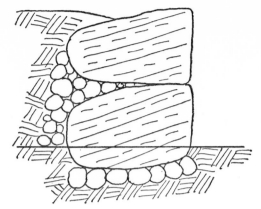

Figure 190.   Arranging stones in tiers.

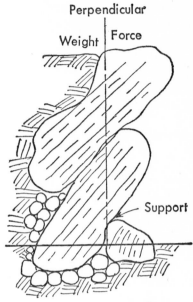

Figure 191.   Cared-in
arrangement.

stones give each other sufficient support. This support is, of course, of great importance when the stones actually touch one another, but even when they are set separated by some distance, maintaining this atmosphere of support is necessary from a mood viewpoint because it gives aesthetic stability.

The gardening beginner, when setting stones of various sizes and shapes, should arrange them mentally first and then go on to the actually placing of the stones one by one. (see *Figures 190* and *191*).

As you see in Figures 192 through 194, when we pile flat-faced stones on each other to make any of a variety of types of walls, the top layer of stones gets lower toward the rear. If this were not so, the top layer would tend to slip and fall down. Some types of wall include the field-stone wall the tortoise-shell pattern, the irregular tortoise shell, and the herringbone pattern.

In Figure 191, in which there is a diagram of the so-called caved-in type setting, you can see that the support stone at the very bottom of the arrangement is set in relation to the two larger upper stones so that its point of support

falls in a direct line with the weight points of the two upper stones and gives them stability. This type of setting has a wide range of applications. All of these caved-in stone settings escape actually caving in through the application of this principle. This use of the principle of leverage is by far stronger against the force of the earth than the field-fence system, or the tortoise-shell-fence system. The hexagonal stone version of the tortoise shell, the irregular tortoise shell, and diamond tortoise shell, are all arranged as you see them in the diagrams. The herringbone and the wicker-work patterns resemble the irregular tortoise shell, but the lines of stones are arranged so that in one row they face in one direction and in the next row in the other. These are practical stone group-

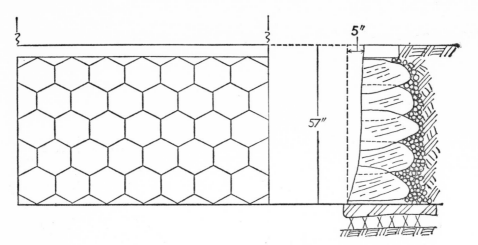

Figure 192.   Hexagonal tortoise-shell pattern.

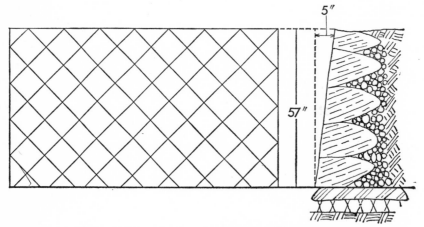

Figure 193.   Diamond tortoise-shell pattern.

ings, but they lack the elegance of the tortoise shell.

As you can see in the cross-section drawings of these stone groupings, behind the wall stones themselves smaller cobble stones (two-eight inches) or pebbles (eight-twelve inches) are packed into the areas between the outer stones then earth is packed in behind that. Usually, if the wall is to be only one yard or less in height there is no need to pack stones behind the wall stones; earth alone will do. However, if there is water drainage behind the stone wall, no matter how low it is, you must use stones, pebbles, and gravel packing. When you use stones and pebbles as packing, you should also use some fine

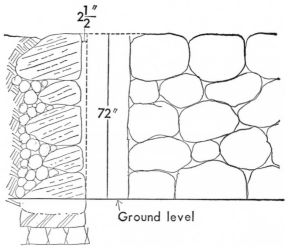

Figure 194.   Irregular tortoise-shell pattern.

sand with them.

When there is a heavy rain and danger

Figure 195.   Front view of procedure in setting stone wall.

that the ground, swollen with rainwater, will push the wall stones out because of the increased side pressure, the stones packed behind the wall stones deflect the soil rainwater in another direction.

Because, when stones are set into the ground, they are likely to become soiled easily, they should be brushed clean of dirt at the end of the day.

Lining up the faces of the stones in a stone wall is done as it is shown in Figure 195. Erect a temporary frame, determine the horizontal, and set the stones so that their surfaces and their heights match. In this type of setting, selecting the stones for the uppermost layer is very important, because, no matter how well the lower stones are set, if the top layer is bad, it will spoil the arrangement. In all cases, flat topped stones are good, but if the top layer stones are too high or too low, some adjustment will have to be made to the stones below them. When you have set three rows of stones, begin to consider the heights and widths of the stones for the top layer. To make it easier to collect the stones for the top layer, guess at the size of the stones in the layer beneath them. In other words, when you have set to the third layer from the top of the wall, choose the top layer stones before choosing the stones for the second layer from the top. Select

the stones for the second layer later, and choose ones that will suit the sizes and widths of the ones you will already have chosen for the upper layer.

In a method directly opposite to that used in the water basin packing stones, where the stones are built up from the bottom, you can, when making a wall of small round stones, set the top layer of stones and put sticks or iron rods of about twelve inches in length under the top stones to support them and keep them from falling. Go on in this fashion until you finish the bottom row of stones, the excess part of which will have to be buried in the ground. Ordinarily, you can economize on work by the proper use of the layer of stones below the top layer, whereas in the case of small stones, the very last layer of stones determines your amount of saved labor.

When setting cobbles or slab stones, you may either use mortar or concrete or you may use plain earth. If you use mortar, however, take care not to let any of it stick to the stones. If some does adhere to the stones, wash it away with a brush before it dries. The usual mortar for the cracks between these stones is one part cement to three parts river sand. These cracks should be deep.

I should now like to mention a few of the points on which you should be careful when working with stepping stones, paving stones, and the *tsukubai* front stone.

When setting stepping stones, first decide on the pitch needed for water drainage, and when the garden ground is well leveled, set the stepping stones temporarily with the thin side to the bottom and the flat area as the upper surface. Try walking on them a number of times, then walk a distance away, and closely examine their appearance. Correct the stones that are difficult to walk on or that do not contribute to the balance of the over-all arrangement as many times as necessary until the arrangement is satisfactory. Then one by one set the stones into the earth by digging holes to suit the thickness of the stones, and put the stones into these holes. Put the stones in this one-by-one way because, if you took them up all at once from their temporary position and then dug all the holes, their positions would change and the original pattern would be destroyed. After you have set the stones, pack earth firmly around their bottoms with a small stick, but keep an eye on the height of the stone from the ground level and on the horizontality of the upper surface, to see that they do not alter.

If you live in an area where the ground freezes in the winter so that there is the danger of the stepping stones' working up out of the ground, dig a four-inch trench that is as unnoticeable as possible along the path the stepping stones follow, and fill the bottom of the trench with sandy soil. Connect this trench with the garden drainage opening.

You may use either mortar or earth to fill the cracks between paving stones, when you are laying them, but use generally mortar only with thin stones, because earth in the cracks between thicker stones gives a more natural feeling.

When you are using mortar, first pour a layer of more than $2\frac{1}{2}$ inches of gravel or sand, then make a foundation of $2\frac{1}{2}$ inches of concrete. On top of this make a coating of mortar (one part cement to three parts river sand) and set the stones as you see them being set in Figure 196. It is more efficient to temporarily line the stones up and make a visual check to see that the stones go together well before coating their bottoms with mortar and setting them.

When the stones are set, coat the cracks with a mortar mixture one part cement to two parts river sand. Instead of coating the cracks, you can also thin the mortar and pour it into the cracks with some spouted container. You can crush the lumps that may form in the mortar and irregularities in the setting with a trowel. Do not forget to wash off with a brush any mortar that might stick to the stones, because leaving this mortar on them will spoil the finished effect. The usual width for the cracks

Figure 196. Setting paving stones.

in paving stones is about ½ inch, but if the stones are larger or smaller, than usual, you may vary the width of the crack to suit them. It is best, however, to maintain a standard average crack width for a beautiful appearance.

The characteristic feature of paving composed of such thin stones as andesite with mortar-filled cracks is the lighthearted feeling the thinness of the stones gives.

Earth-filled cracks are used when we set paving stones of some of the thicker varieties of stones such as granite, diorite, and tufa.

In the case of these paving stones, too, we give consideration to the possibility of their working out of the ground when the ground freezes in winter, by laying more than 2½ inches of sand or gravel under them before we begin the pavement. Fill the cracks with a fine, half-dry soil, cover the soil with *muku-muku-chirimen* moss, and water it. It is all right to plant mosses in the cracks even in strong sunlight. If the place is very sunny you might also plant Japanese phlox or some other flowering plant.

When the pavement has a straight edge, we construct a drainage ditch running along the outline of the pavement and then set the paving stones inward from the edge using the present position and height of the stones as a guide. On the other hand, if the pavement is to have a curved or an irregular edge, we use a level to prevent irregularities in the height of the stones and pave outward toward the edge, giving the outer stones a suitable curve or the proper irregularities.

In Figure 197 you see the drainage hole in front of the *tsukubai* wash basin. This hole should be more than 20 inches deep, and you can determine its shape and size by using something like an inverted flower pot as a guide. The bottom of the hole is covered with cobble stones so that it will retain water well.

The opening at the top of the hole should be about ¾ inch in diameter. Use a long plug of some sort to keep this hole open while you pour the concrete and add a coat of mortar. When the concrete and mortar are dry, cover the bottom of the hole with stones so that the mortar does not show. Because this is a cross-section chart of the basin and the front stones, the other

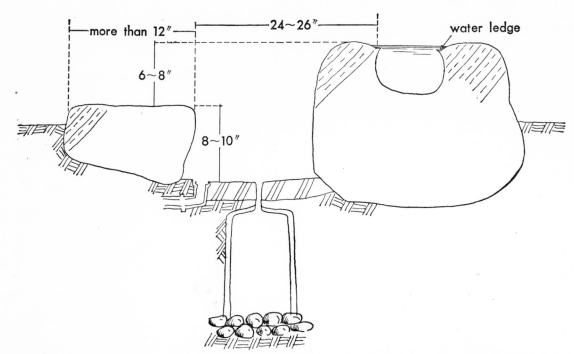

Figure 197.   Cross section of the front arrangement at a tsukubai *and its drainage pit.*

stones in the rear of the basin do not show.

When you use a *kakehi* to supply large quantities of water or even without a *kakehi*, when there is a great deal of rain, water will stand and make the stones in the bottom of the *tsukubai* "sea" dirty. To avoid this make a drainage opening in a suitable place and hide the opening with stones.

§5   *Zigzag and Earthen Bridge Construction*

Although a bridge can become a main feature of the scenery of a garden, when they are sometimes constructed in places where they are not needed, the garden tends to look artificial. It is important to put bridges only where they are needed or, in other words, only where they are inevitable.

It is easy to make a bridge of slightly arched natural stones which have been processed a bit, because these stones could come right from the garden. In addition, such long narrow slab stones as the Nebugawa stone or some types of schist make a good natural rock bridges.

You can also make simple and very refined bridges by splitting logs of a diameter of more than twelve inches and turning the flat side up in a zigzag-bridge fashion, or by constructing an earthen bridge.

As you see in Figure 198, the earthen bridge is constructed by laying two arched slit logs across the stream as crosspieces, then nailing smaller logs (three to four inches in diameter) across the crosspieces so that there are no cracks between the smaller logs. Cut bamboo poles slightly behind the joint and line

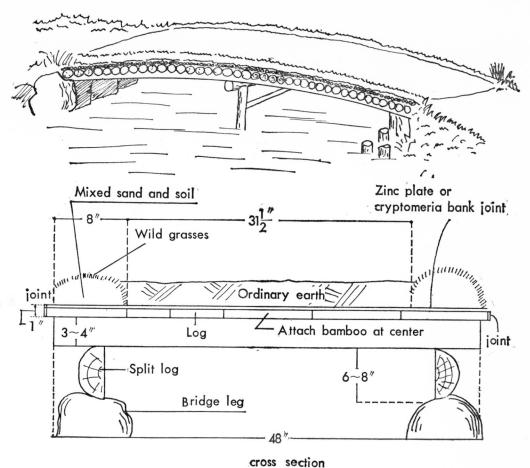

Mixed sand and soil

Zinc plate or cryptomeria bank joint

8″

31½″

Wild grasses

joint

Ordinary earth

1″

3~4″

Log

Attach bamboo at center

joint

Split log

6~8″

Bridge leg

48″

cross section

Figure 198. Earthen bridge.

them up with openings between them. On top of this lay a thin zinc plate, on top of which on either side of the bridge pile semicircular mounds of a mixture of equal parts of fine soil and sand. If the place is shady, you should plant moss, pondweed or some other flowering plant, on these mounds. Spread an equal mixture of fine soil and sand between the two outer earth mounds, and pack it down firmly and evenly. The bamboo is cut so as to end in a joint on both ends. This means that if the joints do not naturally fall so that the bamboo will be the correct length, the pole must be cut and tied together so that it will be doubled at the center. This adds a little extra strength, just to

make sure the bridge is sturdy.

A zigzag bridge looks good in a place where there are iris and flags. We have given several examples of zigzag bridges in the previous section on bridges, but the one in Figure 199 is a particularly simple version. This bridge is constructed of split logs clamped into H-shape legs. It would be more rigid, if you nail supports to the legs beneath the water level. It would also be interesting to line up three chestnut logs in a row and have them cross over hexagonal stones. If you are using planks in place of logs, pasania or oak planks two inches thick and twelve inches wide are dark, refined, and durable. Boards from old ships are also very interesting in this type of

Figure 199. zigzag bridge.

bridge. You could also use natural stones set on a stone platform in curving lines like stepping stones for a refined bridge. The bridge at the Kanazawa Kenroku garden in Ishikawa Prefecture, is an example of this type.

§6   *Flowerbed Construction*

In constructing a flower bed, we usually spread four inches of river sand first, because it provides good drainage. On top of this we spread a two-inch layer of fertilizer, then twelve inches of garden soil. If the bed is for roses, substitute sandy loam or red loam for the garden soil.

It is best to make a border for the flowerbed to create a distinction between it and the other parts of the garden. If there is no border, the flowerbed losses its own character, and an atmosphere of natural flowers in a natural setting becomes primary. Make the border eight or twelve inches wide and plant such low grasses as ribbon grass or phlox in it. You might also use a low border of pruned azaleas, *kusatsuge*, *hakuchoge*, or Chinese juniper. A border of posts or bamboo lined along the edge of the bed, or one of empty bottles or tiles set alternately are also good. If the poles are birch with the white bark still on, they harmonize well with Western-style flowers and with roses. Since wood decays and is a good breeding place for ants, you might prefer to use concrete blocks or bricks in the border.

In Figure 200, you can see some of the various methods of bordering and particularly the wide bordering applications of bricks.

In the long-side setting, the bricks are lined up on the soil with the long side up. This type of setting requires only a few bricks.

The staggered long-side setting, as you can see in the chart, gives a light and nimble feeling.

The small-end setting has the small ends of the bricks arranged up and level so that the sides of the bricks show. Since bricks in this arrangement can be buried deep, it is a secure and stable setting with a settled and comfortable look.

The triangular arrangement is a type of long-side arrangement, in which only a triangular section of the bricks show above the ground. It would, however, be just as good to let the bricks show a little more than they do in the chart.

The zigzag setting, also, is a type of long-side arrangement set in a zigzag line, as you see in the chart.

Another of the long-side arrangements

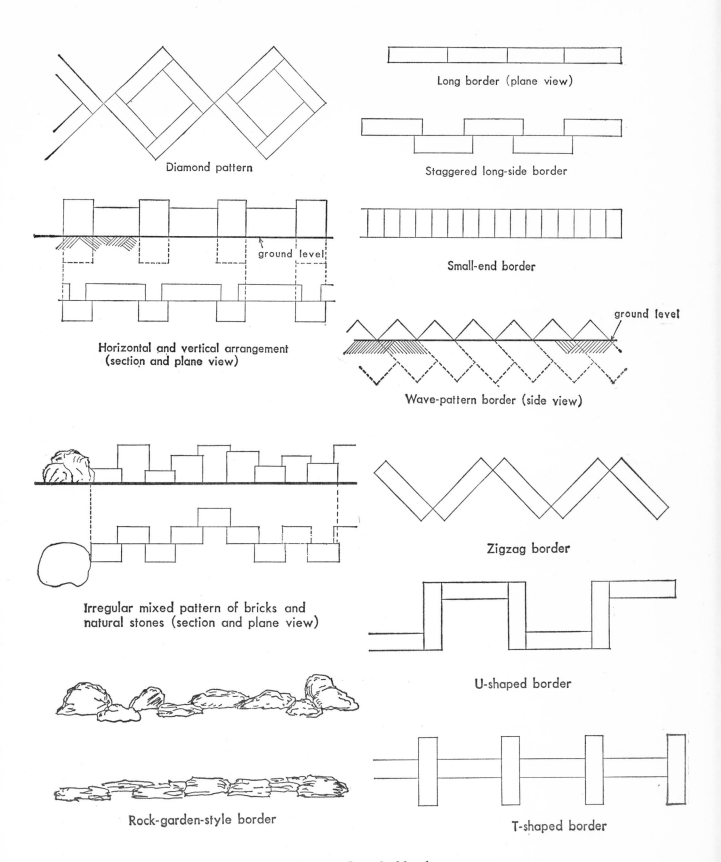

Diamond pattern

Long border (plane view)

Staggered long-side border

ground level

Small-end border

Horizontal and vertical arrangement
(section and plane view)

ground level

Wave-pattern border (side view)

Irregular mixed pattern of bricks and
natural stones (section and plane view)

Zigzag border

U-shaped border

Rock-garden-style border

T-shaped border

Figure 200.   Various flowerbed borders.

is the U shape setting which is also seen in the chart.

The diamond-connection setting is really made up of bricks arranged in squares, but if you look at these squares from an angle, they look like diamond shapes. It is interesting to plant small flowers inside the squares the bricks enclose.

The vertical-horizontal setting has bricks with their long sides up alternating with bricks with their short sides up and provides interesting gradations in height.

There is also a setting in which bricks set at irregular heights but facing flat front are highlighted by natural stones in the border.

Though we have already mentioned ten types of brick borders, there are still various others. The red of the bricks contrasts pleasantly with the bright green leaves of the trees, but spraying or painting them with white paint also makes for a fresh feeling. If you use minerals in your border, use the simplest you can, and change and alter them from time to time for a pleasant feeling.

Recently the number of people who use concrete blocks as borders has grown quite a bit. Although these blocks look crude, their whiteness is refreshing, and they are perfectly all right for anyone who likes them.

A bed of low flowers with a natural rock-garden style border is also interesting, but this type of border does not suit tall plants, which only look messy with the border arrangement.

§7 *Lawn*

Among the Japanese lawns there are field, *naka*, *korai*, and *kitakorai* lawns, all of which are turf lawns whereas among the Western varieties there are such lawns as Kentuky blue grass, Cox Grass, and Highland Best Grass, all of which are grown from seed.

The Japanese varieties look lovelier in the heat of midsummer, and even when they have turned yellow they produce a pleasantly warm feeling. Because they spread well, they are a more advantageous and luxuriant type of lawn. On the other hand sunlight and proper drainage are of prime importance to them. Regardless of how carefully you treat them and fertilize them, they will not grow well if they are not properly drained and do not get the proper amount of sunlight. To make a good lawn, you must plant it in a place where it will get at least five hours of good sun a day.

To insure proper drainage below the level of the lawn, dig up the earth to a depth of 16 inches lower than the surface of the lawn and lay a layer of cobble stones or stones about the size of chestnuts, four inches thick. On top of this make a layer of fine sand or sandy soil four inches thick. If you then put eight inches of garden soil on top of this, draining the lawn properly will be simple. If you substitute charcoal for the stones in the drainage layer to a ratio of about $39\frac{2}{3}$ pounds to 30 square yards, this will not only make for good drainage, but since the charcoal will absorb water, during a time of drought, the roots of the grass can penetrate deep into the charcoal for a supply of moisture.

On the other hand, in areas where there is little rain, make provisions for a sprinkling system before you plant the lawn.

If you use your lawn for golf practice, have your topsoil only six inches deep, and spread your lawn with a level mixture of soil and SCP mixed to a ratio of about $1\frac{1}{2}$ pounds to one square yard to keep the lawn from being trampled to death. If the lawn is already planted, you might roll thoroughly into the surface of the lawn a mixture of garden soil and SCP to a ratio of $4\frac{2}{3}$ ounces to one square yard and break up the top soil to a depth of

about one inch. This should to some extent prevent damage caused by walking on the surface of the lawn.

When planting a Japanese field lawn, remove all of the weeds from the site, prepare the lawn base as we indicated above, and level the top soil carefully. Then lay the turf blocks on top of this so that there is a one-inch crack between the them, and press them down lightly with a board so that the leaves are still showing above the soil in the cracks. If you are planting the lawn on flat ground, secure the turfs with slender sharpened sticks, four to a turf block. If the lawn is on a sharp incline, however, use six sticks to a turf block. When setting the turf blocks on a level site, try to avoid having the cracks between the blocks intersect at right angles. Usually, it is better to have the long side of the turf block more easily visible. If you are planting the turf blocks on a steep incline, however, the long sides of the blocks should be set at right angles against the incline to help hold the root soil of the turf block and to prevent its being washed away in heavy rains. Water the turf blocks after setting them, and continue to water them until it rains.

It will take about 24 turf blocks of Japanese field lawn to plant three square yards. Twenty-four blocks of *korai* lawn will plant about 2.1 square yards, but if you want, you may use the same amount of blocks in three square yards and when the summer has passed, the openings between the blocks will have grown closed. In something like a golf course, where you will want to walk on the turf immediately, set the turf blocks close together with no cracks between them. In an ordinary garden, on the other hand, it is usual to leave $\frac{3}{4}$ to 1 inch between the blocks so that the grass can grow into the area between.

To cut expenses, you might literally stretch the turf blocks out by standing on one end with one foot and pulling on the other end with both hands. You might also cut long narrow holes in the ground and set the turf in strips. If your site is on an incline, you can knead the turf to the consistency of wall plaster and more or less paint the side of the hill with it, but if you do this, it will be two years before the site looks like a lawn.

You may plant the seed for a Western-style lawn anytime from spring to autumn, but autumn planting gives the best results. These seeds, like wheat, produce green plants in the winter, but in the summer they are not as beautiful as Japanese turf lawns.

To sow the seeds, prepare the drainage as we described it in the section on Japanese lawns, fertilize the ground, level and roll the top soil, and prepare a mixture of one part grass seed to three parts sand. We mix the seed with sand, because the seeds are fine, and unless they are thinned with something, they may fall too thick. In addition, if the seed is mixed with sand, it is easier to tell where you have sown and where you have not. In place of sand you might also use a light soil like that used in the cracks between turf blocks.

If the weather is dry after you sow the seed, water the area with a fine-spray hose or with a fine watering can, if you have only seeded a small garden.

Although you cannot transplant Western lawn with only the thin $\frac{1}{2}$ inch of soil on the bottom, as you can with Japanese lawn, you may move some of the turf from places where it is particularly thick, if you are careful to leave a one-inch layer of soil on the roots. Do not forget that it is essential to water the transplanted turf every day.

Because a garden with a lawn that is not too short and that looks something like the lawn on a golf course is lovely, you need cut your grass only once a month from mid-spring till autumn.

By way of lawn care, we would like to mention that to restore roots stalks that have water rot, mix dry sand and ash ($1\frac{1}{3}$ ounces to three square yards) with light soil. If you live in a very humid region, it is effective to sprinkle sand and ash on top of light soil.

Urea fertilizers are very good additional fertilizer for the lawn, but be sure if you use them as they are, to water them once to avoid the danger of chemically damaging the grass.

To remove weeds mix a blend of $1\frac{1}{3}$ ounces of 24D to two liters of water for three square yards of plot, and sprinkle the ground with it.

For such harmful pests as the may-bug, simply spray the lawn from time to time with DDT or BHC. Two pounds of DDT well mixed in one hundred gallons of water sprayed on the lawn until the leaves are thoroughly wet will rid you of may-bugs.

§8　Mosses and Lichens

Some of the types of mosses frequently used in the shady parts of Japanese gardens are the hairmoss, *niwasugi* moss, *eizan* moss, *nishiki* moss, *muku-muku-chirimen* moss, and *hikagenoka-tsura*.

Hairmoss is found in pine groves or in deep mountain forests and has leaves resembling the needles of the cryptomeria. There are other varieties of the hairmoss such as the *hime* hairmoss, and the *seitaka* hairmoss, but the ordinary hairmoss is most often used in gardens. Like turf for the lawn, you can cut hairmoss into blocks about 30 square inches in area and about $\frac{3}{4}$ inch thick and use it that way. It has a very refined color and is quite beautiful. Sweeping the ground with a bamboo broom takes other mosses up, but hairmoss is more tenacious. You can also plant it on the side of an incline and secure it with small sticks to that it does not slide down. *Niwasugi* moss resembles the hairmoss, but it will not stand sweeping the way

the true hairmoss will.

When you are planting hairmoss, sweep the ground first and remove all useless weeds by the roots. Then plant the moss around the bases of the trees and stones. Plant the moss by softening and watering the ground till it is muddy and lightly pressing the moss down with your hands. A few days after you have planted the moss, fill in the cracks with light soil as you did in the case of lawn planting so that the edges of the moss you planted are covered.

Eizan moss can also be transplanted in blocks with soil, but it can also be pulled and stretched out with both hands and then set into muddy soil, so that light filling soil is unnecessary. It is good to hide the edges of stepping stones with *eizan* moss, but if there are fallen leaves which you must sweep away, be careful, because the moss, will get twisted in the leaves and will come up with them. In addition, this moss sometimes seems to pall and disappear, then when you have given up on it, it will come out again. Though it has these failings, because it is easy to grow and beautiful, it is even more widely used in gardens than hairmoss. To plant this moss, stretch it out with both hands and press it into muddy soil. If your moss is scarce, cut it into small pieces, and stick it into the ground at two-inch intervals, and it will take root and thrive.

Nishiki moss resembles *eizan* moss to the extent that it is sometimes called by the same name, but because it turns a reddish color in the winter the *nishiki* (two-colored) has been applied to it. It is planted the same way that *eizan* moss is. Although mixing this moss in a natural way with hairmoss is very pretty, the *nishiki* moss creeps up over the hairmoss and injures it. It is better to use the *nishiki* moss in a place for which you have no other use.

Because *niwasugi* moss breaks apart and scatters easily it is difficult to care for, but if it is pressed into muddy soil it will grow. *Niwasugi* moss that has come up naturally will not come up easily, even when it is swept, and gives the true feeling of a moss garden.

Hairmoss is beautiful and is very nice planted around shrubbery or mixed in a sort of design in among some *muku-muku-chirimen* moss, but if you make an entire flat area in a garden into a hair-moss plot, the moss will grow too tall and will look messy. It is much more attractive to use mainly *muku-muku-chirimen* moss and add designs of hairmoss or *eizan* moss. Planting *muku-muku-chirimen* moss is very easy; you only have to water the surface of the ground and lay the moss on top of it.

There are certain types of moss like the *zeni* moss and the *ja* moss that fit the surface of the ground exactly, but since these mosses are not only difficult to plant, but may also damage the other mosses, if they appear, it is best to get rid of them.

Though *hikagenokatsura* is very beautiful with its long slender roots as it climbs over rocks and trees, it is not often used as a ground covering. It is, however, interesting to use this moss in the center of other mosses as an accessory. It is planted the same way *eizan* moss is.

Pondweeds can be planted in large clumps, but it can also be cut into small pieces and put into holes that are about four inches apart. If you plant it this way, it will cover the whole area in two to three years.

Himesekisho should be planted in an arid region. It looks nice between rocks, but if it is planted near water or in a bright place it should be set with the leaves facing in a natural way. This moss will not rot even if you separate the roots when you plant it. You will be able to tell the underside of the leaf from the top because the top is more lusterous. Plant the moss so that the tops of the leaves face up. If you are symbolizing water, it is good to use the long *sekisho* or the one with a middle-sized leaf. The ordinary *sekisho* does not make a good ground cover because it gets to look dirty.

Be sure to plant the fringed iris so that its shiny leaves will be up, and face it toward the water to get the real feeling of the plant.

When you bring *yabukoji* from the mountains, make a bunch of several stalks of it and plant it temporarily. When the new leaves come out line the leaves up properly and plant the stalks you want to plant. This is a much simpler method than planting them one by one just after you bring them home.

Pink reineckia just like *yabukoji* is difficult to plant because the leaves must be turned in a natural way. It is easier and more efficient to make a cutting of this anytime between mid-spring and summer. If this plant is unskilfully planted it will look as if it has been trampled down and will be unsightly.

Because the bamboo grasses will rot without their underground roots, be sure to dig the roots up with them. When selecting grasses, choose the ones whose roots look shallow when you have cleared away the surrounding plants, because this type will take transplanting well. Trees and plants bought at a nursery have been moved once and have developed good roots. If you look at the plant and its leaves are firmly set, it has been transplanted once and may be used safely.

If the grasses are too high they will also be too thick and will cease to look like a ground cover. Since the upper shoots come out in the early summer, prune them then from the root base, then let the second new buds come out to keep the plants short.

In early summer, when the ferns have already put out leaves once which are set firmly and the second buds have appeared, they make a really beautiful ground cover. Using them as base plants for stones, also, looks pleasant and shows how many ways the ferns can be used.

When using other low plants, clip them close in early summer, and they will grow better and look lovelier.

AUTHOR'S NOTE

THE EDITORIAL STAFF *of the publisher of this book, in an attempt to make Japanese garden techniques as easy to understand as possible from the reader's viewpoint, and also in an effort to create an effective narrative, have made a number of changes in the order and arrangement of the materials of the book, all with my agreement. In addition, since things that are easy enough to understand in Japanese, require some effort to make understandable in English, the translator conferred with me on all doubtful points, and I feel that there is no cause for concern on this score.*

Those of us who live everday submerged in the art of gardening, have a tendency to overlook things that are of vital interest to the general reader, because these points are our everyday fare. For this reason, I feel that there are many instances in which the author and the reader of garden books have no chance to really get together. Although I too have committed this error in the past, in the present book I believe that the efforts made to vividly convey our meaning to the reader are apparent. On this point I am deeply grateful to the editorial staff and to the English translation.

If this book, published as a result of all these efforts, brings an understanding to people of other countries of, not merely the refinement of the tea garden, which everyone understands, but also of the light elegance and the mysterious covering of splendid things with a veil of refinement, these people will become graduates of the art of Japanese gardening. With the hope that there will be many such people, I now lay down my pen.

The Author

Tokyo, October, 1964

APPENDIX

Garden Trees and Plants in This Book

JAPANESE NAME	BOTANICAL NAME	ENGLISH NAME
A		
Akamatsu	*Pinus densiflora*	Japanese red pine
(Akame)yamazakura	*Prunus donarium*	
Aoki	*Aucuba japonica*	Japanese aucuba
Arakashi	*Quercus Glauca*	Ring-cupped oak
Asebo	*Pieris japonica*	
Atsumoriso	*Cypripedium Thunbergii*	
B		
Basho	*Musa Basjoo*	Japanese banana
Benishida	*Dryopteris erythrosora*	
Biwa	*Eriobotrya japonica*	Loquat
Boke	*Chaenomeles lagenaria*	
Botan	*Paeonia suffruticosa*	Peony
Bungozasa	*Shibataea Kumasasa*	
D		
Daimyochiku	*Semiarundinaria fastuosa*	Daimyo bamboo
(Dai)sugi	*Cryptomeria japonica*	Japanese cedar
Dodan	*Enkianthus perulatus*	
E		
Eizangoke	*Selaginella japonica*	
F		
Fuyo	*Hibiscus mutabilis*	Rose mallow
G		
Gaku	*Hydrangea scandens*	
Gamazumi	*Viburnum dilatatum*	
Goyomatsu	*Pinus pentaphylla*	Japanese white pine
Gonzui	*Euscaphis japonica*	
H		
Hagi	*Lespedeza bicolor*	Bush clover
Hakuchoge	*Serissa japonica*	
Hanashobu	*Iris ensata*	Sweet flag
Haran	*Aspidistra elatior*	Aspidistra
Hiba	*Chamaecyparis pisifera*	
Hiiragi	*Osmanthus aquifolium*	
Hiiraginanten	*Mahonia japonica*	
Hikagenokazura	*Lycopodium clavatum*	
(Hime)mizuki	*Cornus controversa*	
(Hime)sekisho	*Acorus gramineus*	
(Hime)sugigoke	*Polytrichum commune*	
(Hime)ashi	*Phragmites communis*	Small reed
Hinoki	*Chamaecyparis obtusa*	White cedar
Hisakagi	*Eurya japonica*	
Horashinobu	*Sphenomeris chusana*	

Japanese Name	Botanical Name	English Name
I		
Ibuki	*Juniperus Chinensis*	Chinese juniper
Ichii	*Taxus cuspidata*	Japanese yew
Icho	*Ginkgo biloba*	Ginkgo tree
Iwabenkei	*Sedum Rhodiola*	Rose root
J		
Jyagoke	*Conocephalum conicum*	*Jya* moss
Jinchoge	*Daphne odora*	Daphne
K		
Kaede	*Acer palmatum*	Maple tree
Kaido	*Malus Halliana*	
Kakuremino	*Gilibertia trifida*	
Kakitsubata	*Iris laevigata*	Iris
Kanikomori	*Cacalia adenostyloides*	
Kanchiku	*Chimons bambusa marmorea*	*Kan* bamboo
Kashiwa	*Quercus dentata*	Daimyo oak
Kaya	*Torreya nucifera*	Japanese torreya
Keyaki	*Zelkova serrata*	Keyaki
(Kinu)koraishiba	*Zoysia tenuifolia*	*Kinukorai* lawn
Kichijiso	*Pachysandra terminalis*	
Kinmasaki	*Aureo-marginata*	
Kirishima	*Rhododendron obtusum*	
Kodemari	*Spiraea cantoniensis*	Reeves spiraea
Kometsuga	*Tsuga diversifolia*	
Kokumazasa	*Sasa albo-marginata*	
Konara	*Quercus glandulifera*	
Koraishiba	*Zyosia japonica*	*Korai* lawn
Kumazasa	*Bambusa Sasa albo-marginata*	Low striped bamboo
Kuri	*Castanea pubinervis*	Japanese chest-nut
Kuroganemochi	*Ilex rotunda*	
Kuromatsu	*Pinus Thunbergii*	Black pine
Kuramagoke	*Selaginella japonica*	
Kusatsuge	*Buxus microphylla*	
Kusu	*Cinnamomum camphora*	Camphor tree
Kumagaiso	*Cypripedium japonicum*	
Kyara	*Taxus cuspidata*	Japanese yew
M		
Maki	*Podocarpus macrophylla*	Chinese black pine
Manryo	*Ardisia crispa*	Spear flower
Mansaku	*Hamamelis japonica*	Japanese witch hazel
Masaki	*Euonymus japonica*	Evergreen burning bush
Matsurika	*Jasminum Sambac*	
Mokkoku	*Ternstroemia japonica*	Arabian jasmine
Mokusei	*Osmanthus fragrans*	Fragrant olive
Momi	*Abies firma*	*Momi* fir
Momiji	*Acer palmatum*	Maple tree
Mosotake	*Phyllostachys edulis*	*Moso* bamboo
Mukumuku-chirimen-goke	*Stereodon plumaeformis*	*Mukumuku-chirimen* moss
Murasakishikibu	*Callicarpa japonica*	Japanese beauty-berry
N		
Nanakamado	*Sorbus commixta*	
Nanten	*Nandina domestica*	Nandina
Narihiradake	*Semiarundinaria fastuosa*	*Narihira* bamboo
Natsuhaze	*Vaccinium oldhami*	
Nikkokisuge	*Hemerocallis Middendorffii*	

Japanese Name	Botanical Name	English Name
Nishikigi	*Euonymus alata*	Winged spindle tree
(Niwa)sugigoke	*Pogonatum contortum*	*Niwasugi* moss
Niwatoko	*Sambucus Sieboldiana*	Elder
(No)shiba	*Zoysia japonica*	Field lawn
O		
Okamezasa	*Shibataea Kumasasa*	Bamboo grass
Omura(saki)	*Rhododendron pulchrum*	
R		
Robai	*Meratia praecox*	Winter jasmine
S		
Saishin	*Asarum Sieboldi*	
Sakura	*Prunus Yedoensis*	Cherry tree
Sarusuberi	*Lagers troemia Indica*	Crape myrtle
Satsuki	*Rhododendron indicum*	Azalea
Sawara	*Chamaecyparis pisifera*	*Sawara* cypress
Seitakasugigoke	*Pogonatum grandifolium*	*Seitakasugi* moss
Sekisho	*Acorus gramineus*	Sweet rush
Shaga	*Iris japonica*	Fringed iris
Shakunage	*Rhododendron Metternichii*	
Shakuyaku	*Paeonia albiflora*	Chinese peony
Sharinbai	*Rhaphiolepis umbellata*	Raphiolepis
Shidareyanagi	*Salix babylonica*	Weeping willow
Shichiku	*Phyllostachys nigra*	Square bamboo
Shidezakura	*Amelanchier Asiatica*	
Shihochiku	*Chimonobambusa quadrangularis*	*Shiho* bamboo
Shii	*Pasania cuspidata*	Pasania
Shirakaba	*Betula platyphylla*	
Shuro	*Trachycarpus Fortunei*	Windmill palm
Sonare	*Juniperus procumbens*	Japanese juniper
Soro	*Carpinus laxiflora*	
Sotetsu	*Cycas revoluta*	Japanese sago palm
Sugi	*Cryptomeria japonica*	Japanese cedar
Sugigoke	*Polytrichum commune*	Hairmoss
Suiren	*Ninphaea Tetragona*	Water lily
Susuki	*Miscanthus sinesis*	Eulalia
T		
Tabu	*Machilus Thunbergii*	
Tachibana	*Ardisia punctata*	
Taiminchiku	*Pleioblastus gramineus*	*Taimin* bamboo
Taisanboku	*Magnolia grandiflora*	Bull bay
Tamasudare	*Zephyranthes candida*	
Tobera	*Pittosporum Tobira*	Japanese pittosporum
Tochi	*Aesculus turbinata*	Japanese horse chestnut
Todomatsu	*Abies Mariesii*	Japanese white pine
Tokaede	*Acer Buergerianum*	Trident maple
Tokusa	*Equisetum hiemale*	
Tsubaki	*Camellia japonica*	Camellia
Tsutsuji	*Rhododendron Variety*	Azalea
Tsuwabuki	*Ligularia tussilaginea*	
U		
Ume	*Prunus Mume*	Japanese apricot
Umemodoki	*Ilex Serrata*	Fine-tooth holly
Utsugi (Unohana)	*Deutzia crenata*	

Japanese Name	Botanical Name	English Name
W		
Wabisuke	*Wabisuke Makino*	Judith
Y		
Yabukoji	*Pseudosasa japonica*	
Yabusotetsu	*Myrica rubra*	
Yadake	*Ardisia japonica*	Arrow bamboo
Yamamomo	*Blechnum niponicum*	Bayberry
Yamatsutsuji	*Rhododendron obtusum*	Torch azalea
Yashi	*Cocos Nucifera*	
Yatsude	*Fatsia japonica*	Japanese aralia
Z		
Zakuro	*Punica Granatum*	Pomegranate
Zenigoke	*Marchantia Polymorpha*	*Zeni* moss

GLOSSARY

bonji—the characters, developed in ancient India, with which Sanscrit is written.

chiri-ana—a round or square hole in the tea garden that is designed to be a place in which to discard the soiled things from the soul.

Edo period—a period in Japanese history named for Edo, the old name for Tokyo, and lasting from 1600 to 1867.

enseishuku **shape**—the letter *en* indicates that this *tsukubai* is round; the letters *seishuku* mean constellation, or the places where the stars dwell. This basin is so named because the stars of the night sky reflect in the water in the conical basin and give the impression that they are actually in the water.

gogyo—the five basic elements, wood, fire, earth, gold, and water, which, according to ancient Chinese learning, were the basic causal factors in the universe and in human life.

gorin **tower**—a tower that is divided into five rings (*gorin*) each of which is designated by one of the five elements: sky, wind, fire, water, and earth.

hanto—the tea ceremony host's assistant.

haori—a short Japanese coat with a lapel worn over the kimono.

Heian period—the period of about 400 years (794–1192) when Kyoto, as the capital of Japan, experienced a rich flowering of the arts.

hin-**shape**—a stone arrangement that resembles the Chinese character 品, *hin*.

kakehi—a pipe to bring water above the surface of the ground.

Kato Kiyomasa—(1562–1611) an outstanding general of the Azuchi Momoyama period (1568–1598) who built Nagoya Castle.

kikyaku **stone**—in the stone classification chart, the stone that is low and stable like the earth.

meji—the crack between paved stones, bricks, or tile.

Meiji—a Japanese historical period that lasted from 1868–1912. It is named for the Emperor Meiji.

mizuage **stone**—a stone to stand on when changing the water in the water basin.

mizukumi **stone**—a low flat stone in front of the water basin on which a man of rank would stand when rinsing his hands.

nachi—a hard black clay stone.

nijiriguchi—a small entranceway, peculiar to the teahouse, that everyone except the most noble guests must use to enter and exit. In order to come in through this entranceway one must edge forward (*nijiru*), and this gives the doorway its name.

Omote senke—a school of the tea ceremony.

reisho **stone**—in the stone classification chart, the stone that, like gold and iron, has a stable form.

roji—an alleyway, also a name for the tea garden.

Sakuteiki—the oldest extant work on Japanese gardening (twelfth century) written by Toshitsuna Tachibana.

sanko **style**—a stone lantern shape that bears carvings of the three lights (*sanko*) the sun, the moon, and the stars.

Sen-no Rikyu—(1522–1591) the most outstanding tea master of the Azuchi Momoyama period (1568–1598).

shibusa—(also *shibui*, or *shibumi*) the opposite of gaudy, elegantly refined. A quiet composure with a taste of profundity.

shigyo **stone**—in the stone classification chart, the stone that branches to the sides, like fire, and indicates spiritual force.

Shin, gyo, so—in relationship to things, the most natural method of using them is called *shin*, the most abbreviated is called *so*, and the method that falls between these two is called *gyo*. These categories apply to a variety of fields including, Japanese characters, calligraphy, and flower arranging.

shin-**shape**—a shape that resembles the Chinese character 心, *shin*.

shintai **stone**—a flat stone that suggests the expanses of water.

Shirawkawa gravel—a white gravel composed of pyroxene and andesite.

Shumisen—(Mount Shumisen) the tall mountain that, according to Buddhist cosmology, rises up in the center of the world.

sozu—A type of clapper used in the fields to chase away deer. When it is used with a *kakehi* flume it makes a resounding noise as it flips downward to pour out the water that has accumulated in it.

sukiya zukuri—architectural style found in teahouses. A peculiarly Japanese architectural style that developed around the needs of the tea ceremony.

taido stone—in the stone classification chart, the stone that rises straight and tall like the trees and indicates nobility.

tanjaku-shape—rectangular like *tanjaku*, a thin paper used for writing or as a tag for tying to other things.

teshoku stone—a stone in front of the *tsukubai* on which to place a light.

Tochotocho Hihikume—a stone arrangement type that is described in the *Sakuteiki* and symbolizes spiritual force.

Tokugawa Mitsukuni—(1628–1700) a shogun and a first-rate historian of the Edo period.

tsukubai—a low water basin. The name is derived from the Japanese word *tsukubau*, which means to crouch, because one must crouch down to use this basin.

yuoke stone—a stone in front of the *tsukubai* on which to place a bucket of hot water for use in winter.

BIBLIOGRAPHY

§1 *Classics on Japanese Gardening*

Tᴀᴄʜɪʙᴀɴᴀ Toshitsuna 橘　　俊　綱	*Sakutei-ki* 作 庭 記	12 century
Zoen 増圓	*Sansui-Narabini-Yakei-Zu* 山 水 并 野 形 図	12 century
Cʜᴜɴᴀɢᴏɴ Yasuhira 中 納 言 康 平	*Sansui-Hiden-Sho* 山 水 秘 傳 抄	14 century
Hɪsʜɪᴋᴀᴡᴀ Moronobu 菱 川 師 宣	*Yokeitsukuri-Niwa-no-Zu* 余 景 作 り 庭 の 図	1633
Kɪᴛᴀᴍᴜʀᴀ Enkin 北 村 援 琴	*Tsukiyama-Teizo-Den* 築 山 庭 造 傳	1736
Aᴋɪsᴀᴛᴏ Ritoken 秋 里 籬 島 軒	*Miyako-Rinsen-Meisho-Zuye* 都 林 泉 名 勝 図 絵	1800
Aᴋɪsᴀᴛᴏ Ritoken 秋 里 籬 島 軒	*Tsukiyama-Teizo-Den*, Part 1 築 山 庭 造 傳 前 編	1829
Aᴋɪsᴀᴛᴏ Ritoken 秋 里 籬 島 軒	*Tsukiyama-Teizo-Den*, Part 2 築 山 庭 造 傳 後 編	1829
(The author is unknown.)	*Tsukiyama-Sansui-Den* 築 山 山 水 傳	1838
Gᴏᴋʏᴏɢᴏᴋᴜ Kakuo 後 京 極	*Sakutei-Ki* (Manuscript) 作 　 庭 　 記	1838
Yᴏᴋᴏɪ Tokifuyu 横 井 時 冬	*Engei-Ko* 園 藝 考	1891
Hᴏɴᴅᴀ Kinkichiro 本 多 錦 吉 郎	*Zukai-Teizo-Ho* 図 解 庭 造 法	1891
Tᴀᴋᴀᴛsᴜ Chugoro 高 津 忠 五 郎	*Tsukiyama-Sansui-Teizo-Hiden* 築 山 山 水 庭 造 祕 傳	1892

§2 *Books in English on Japanese Gardens* (In order of publication date)

Cᴏɴᴅᴇʀ, Josiah.	*Landscape Gardening in Japan.* 164p, 37 ils, Kelly & Walsh, Tokyo, 1893.
Aᴋɪʏᴀᴍᴀ, Aisaburo.	*Pagodas in Sunrise Land.* 116p, Akiyama, Tokyo, 1915.
Hᴀʀᴀᴅᴀ, Jiro.	*The Gardens of Japan.* 180p, 216 ils, Studio, London, 1928.
Japanese Government Railways.	*Japanese Landscape Gardens.* 64p, 45 ils, Tokyo, 1926.
Lᴇᴇ, Guy H.	*Japanese Gardens.* 48p, Boston, 1935.
Sʜɪɢᴀ, Naoya & Hᴀsʜɪᴍᴏᴛᴏ, Motoshi. ed.	*Gardens of Japan.* 184p, 150 ils, Zauho, Tokyo, 1935.
Sʜᴇʀʀɪʟʟ, Charles H.	*Some Old Kyoto Gardens and Their Thought.* 16p, K.B.S., Tokyo, 1935.
Kᴜᴄᴋ, Loraine, E.	*One Hundred Kyoto Gardens.* 144p, 75 ils, Thompson, Kobe, 1935.
Sɴᴇʟʟ, Fanny Carpenter.	*Moods of a Japanese Garden.* 84p, 32 ils, Dorrance, Philadelphia, 1935.
Tᴀᴍᴜʀᴀ, Tsuyoshi.	*Art of the Landscape Garden in Japan.* 246p, 193 ils, K.B.S., Tokyo, 1936.
Nᴇᴡsᴏᴍ, Samuel.	*Japanese Gardens.* 12p, K.B.S., Tokyo, 1937.
Nᴇᴡsᴏᴍ, Samuel.	*Japanese Garden Construction.* 302p, 270 ils, Wabun-sha, Tokyo, 1939.
Kᴜᴄᴋ, Loraine, E.	*The Art of Japanese Gardens.* 304p, 67 ils, John Day, New York, 1940.
Hᴀʀᴀᴅᴀ, Jiro, Nᴏᴍᴀ, Seiroku, and others.	*Masterpieces of Japanese Art., Vol. II: Architecture and Gardens.* 21p, 69il, Central Federation of Nippon Culture, Tokyo, 1944.
Nɪsʜɪᴍᴜʀᴀ, Tei.	*Country Gardens.* 138p, 82 ils, Bijutsu Shuppan-sha, Tokyo, 1953.
Nᴇᴡsᴏᴍ, Samuel.	*A Thousand Years of Japanese Gardens.* 318p, 280 ils, Tokyo News Service, Tokyo, 1953.
Kɪᴛᴀᴏ, Harumichi.	*Teahouse Gardens.* Shokoku-sha, Tokyo, 1954.
Hᴀʀᴀᴅᴀ, Jiro.	*Japanese Gardens.* 160p, Bradford, Boston, 1956.
Kᴜʙᴏ, Tadashi.	*"An oldest note of secrets on Japanese gardens: A compilation of the 'Sakutei-ki'",* Bulletin of Osaka Prefectural University, Series, Vol. 6, 1956.
Sʜɪɢᴇᴍᴏʀɪ, Kanto.	*The Artistic Garden of Japan in 3 Vols.* each 124p (il), Riko Tosho, Tokyo, 1957.

NISHIMURA, Tei.   *Gardens and Teahouses.* 220p, 99 ils, Kodan-sha, Tokyo, 1957.

OKA, Minoru.   *Short Pageant of Japanese Art, Vol. VI: Architecture and Gardens.* 177p, 50 ils, Tuttle, Tokyo, 1957.

YOSHIDA, Tetsuro.   *Gardens of Japan.* il, Draeger, 1957.

ISHIMOTO, Tatsuo.   *The Art of the Japanese Garden,* 128p, 169 ils, Crown, New York, 1958.

YOSHINAGA, Yoshinobu.   *Japanese Traditional Gardens.* 212p, 144 ils, Shokoku-sha, Tokyo, 1958.

YOSHINAGA, Yoshinobu.   *Composition and Expression in Japanese Traditional Gardens.* 195p, 162 ils, Tokyo, 1958.

TAKAKUWA, Gisei.   *Gardens of Japan.* 108p (il), Mitsumura Suiko Shoin, Tokyo, 1958.

KITAO, Harumichi.   *Formation of Bamboo,* 131p, 132 ils, Shokoku-sha, Tokyo, 1958.

KITAO, Harumichi.   *Formation of Stone,* 138p, 131 ils, Shokoku-sha, Tokyo, 1958.

ENGEL, David H.   *Japanese Gardens for Today.* 272p, 279 ils, Tuttle, Tokyo, 1959.

SHIGEMORI, Kanto & NEWSOM, Samuel.   *Japanese Gardens.* 196p, 157 ils, Tokyo News Service, Tokyo, 1960.

GROPIUS, Walter, TANGE, Kenzo, & ISHIMOTO, Yasuhiro.   *Katsura,* 230p, 144 ils, Zokei-sha, Tokyo, 1960.

TAKAKUWA, Gisei.   *Invitation to Japanese Gardens.* 84p, 158 ils, Mitsumura Suiko Shoin, Tokyo, 1960.

TAKAKUWA, Gisei.   *The Zen Gardens. Vol.* 2, each 108p (il), Mitsumura Suiko Shoin Tokyo, 1960.

SAITO, Katsuo.   *Designing Japanese Gardens.* 230p, 476 ils, Gihodo, Tokyo, 1961.

TATSUI, Matsunosuke.   *Japanese Gardens,* 12th ed., 100p, 59 ils, JTB, Tokyo, 1961.

HORIGUCHI, Sutemi, KOJIRO, Yuichiro, and HAMAGUCHI, Ryuichi.   *Tradition of Japanese Gardens.* 188p, 140 ils, K.B.S., Tokyo, 1962.

MORI, Osamu.   *Typical Japanese Gardens.* 161p, 155il, Shibata-shoten, Tokyo, 1962.

KASHIKIE, Isamu.   *The ABC of Japanese Gardening.* 64p, 53 ils, JPT, Tokyo, 1964.